BEST PRACTICES IN QUANTITATIVE METHODS FOR DEVELOPMENTALISTS

Kathleen McCartney
Margaret R. Burchinal
Kristen L. Bub

Willis F. Overton
Series Editor
W. Andrew Collins
Co-editor

MONOGRAPHS OF THE SOCIETY FOR RESEARCH IN CHILD DEVELOPMENT

Serial No. 285, Vol. 71, No. 3, 2006

 **Blackwell**
Publishing

Boston, Massachusetts   Oxford, United Kingdom

BEST PRACTICES IN QUANTITATIVE METHODS FOR DEVELOPMENTALISTS

CONTENTS

EDITORS' PREFACE

Estimates of progress in any field of study rightly emphasize the research questions and findings that mark advances over the preoccupations of previous periods. In the case of contemporary developmental science, progress would take account of earlier contrasts to such topics as brain development and interrelations with emotion, cognition, and behavior; the biological bases of disorders; the significance of close relationships in developmental context; and a focus on individual and social regulatory processes. Some of these advances reflect or lead innovations and advances that are also evident in other fields. Other recent directions stem from changing societal preoccupations (e.g., Cairns, 1998/2006). As a case in point, Kagan (1992) observed that interest in attachment theory rose with the steady increase in the number of working mothers and the corresponding increase in alternate forms of child care.

In contrast, research methods and statistical tools often are regarded as canonical and relatively stable. True enough, classic methods such as observation and experimentation remain robust foundations for what scientists do and what they learn. Historically, however, a degree of flux has occurred in the forms and contexts in which such mainstays appear. In Mussen's (1963) *Handbook of Research Methods in Child Development*, the methodological fountainhead for the generation of scholars now approaching retirement, these two methods appeared together under the section heading "General Research Methodology in Child Development." Much of the rest of the volume consisted of accounts of the application of observational and experimental methods in specific sub-areas of the field: perception (E. Gibson & Olum), learning (Spiker), group behavior (Thompson), and interpersonal behavior (Lambert). Other chapters provided a mix of traditional and several non-traditional topics: methods for interviewing children (L. Yarrow), the *méthode clinique* of Jean Piaget (Inhelder & Matalon), psycholinguistic methods (Berko & Brown), projective techniques (Henry), standardized tests measuring abilities (Anastasi), attitudes and values (M. R. Yarrow), personality characteristics (Bronfenbrenner &

Ricciuti), and motivation and affect (Miller). Understandably, forerunners of today's sophisticated research on biological processes are harder to detect, though the interest is represented by chapters on studying physical growth (Meredith), "chemical and physiological growth" (Macy & Kelly), and receptor functions (Reisen). Only two chapters focused on the measurement of contexts—ethnographic methods (Whiting & Whiting) and the measurement of family-life variables (L. W. Hoffman & R. Lippitt). In short, Mussen's volume faithfully represented the methodological traditions and the emphasis on rigorous assessment that had been laboriously established in the 1920s and 1930s when the field was striving for scientific respectability vis à vis experimental psychology.

Today, researchers have either expanded the number and variety of laboratory techniques—or have moved into new spheres altogether. Though honoring traditional commitments to disciplined inquiry, new methodological forms have entered the research process, from design to statistical analysis. (Only the forms in which results are reported have remained largely unchanged—a topic that currently occasions considerable ferment.) This sea change has left many of today's mid-career scientists perpetually feeling the need to update their knowledge. Moreover, as the introductory chapter of this monograph makes clear, even many more recently trained developmentalists also grapple with the rapid pace of advances. Members of both groups frequently note that the velocity and the scope of methodological changes presents challenges in their research and/or in their ongoing roles as consumers of knowledge.

This monograph is a timely response to these concerns. The editors of the monograph, Kathleen McCartney, Margaret Burchinal, and Kristen Bub, aim to provide an overview of currently salient topics and issues in developmental methodology. Located somewhere between primer and handbook, the resulting collection of chapters can be used as a scaffold for students and a source of replenishment for more knowledgeable practicing developmentalists. The editors and chapter authors provide both a contemporary take on staple topics (e.g., sampling, psychometrics, correlational methods) and a conceptual introduction to newer, highly sophisticated methods such as Growth Curve Analysis and handling missing data. The initial chapter is a practical guide to recommended data management practices, and the concluding chapter offers a perspective on the practical importance of research findings. The monograph is not, nor was it intended to be, the complete treatise on the state of developmental methodology. Rather, it is an accessible entry point for those who want and need to know more about the growing methodological repertoire available to developmental scientists.

From the perspective of the field in general and the monographs in particular, this monograph appears at a propitious time. It is the final issue in the six-year series produced during the editorship of Willis F. Overton. To acknowledge its transitional position, Overton and the editor-designate W. Andrew Collins, whose term begins with the April 2007 issue, served as joint editors of the issue. Underscoring the evolving methodology that characterizes high-quality research on children and development is a fitting marker of the editorial transition and an avowal of the continuing commitment of both monographs and the Society for Research in Child Development to advancing rigorous and forward-looking research in developmental science.

REFERENCES

Cairns, R. B. (1998/2006). The making of developmental psychology. In W. Damon (Series Ed.). R. M. Lerner (Vol. Ed.), *Handbook of child psychology. Vol. 1: History and systems of developmental psychology* (pp. 25–105). New York: Wiley.

Kagan, J. (1992). Yesterday's premises, tomorrow's promises. *Developmental Psychology*, 28, 990–997.

Mussen, P. H. (Ed.). (1963). *Handbook of research methods in child development.* New York: Wiley.

—*W. Andrew Collins*
—*Willis F. Overton*

INTRODUCTION TO THE MONOGRAPH

The role of quantitative methods in testing developmental hypotheses is widely recognized, yet even very experienced quantitative researchers often lack the knowledge required for good decision making on methodology. The main reason for this is that methodological papers are often too technical to be accessible to social scientists. Not surprisingly, methodologists write primarily for methodologists. Even when methodologists, committed to translating state of the art methods for practitioners, write textbooks, it is often difficult for researchers to comprehend and master new practices. We do not believe that there is one single stumbling block to learning new methods; instead, our colleagues cite a plethora of factors, including lack of institutional resources and support, limited time, low frustration tolerance, and formulae phobia. The end result is a disconnect between research and practice in methods. As such, developmental researchers sometimes use less advanced, less powerful, and less appropriate methods than are available.

The purpose of this monograph is to fill a gap in the literature by offering a series of overviews on common data-analytic issues of particular interest to researchers in child development. Most guides and books focus narrowly on a given topic (e.g., multiple regression) to provide depth. In this monograph, our goal is to provide breadth, beginning with data management and ending with data interpretation. We view this monograph as a first step to getting quantitative researchers started. In every chapter, the authors refer their readers to additional resources for further study. The end result is a reference that we believe will help researchers make better informed decisions about methodology. Although most of the material is not developmental per se, the techniques selected for review are and will continue to be of interest to developmentalists.

The idea for this monograph emerged at the 2005 Biennial Meeting of the Society for Research in Child Development (SRCD), held in Atlanta. As Co-Chairs of the Program Committee, Roger Bakeman and Kathleen McCartney initiated a series of "Back-to-School" workshops. The first set focused on methods and included an invited symposium on practices in

1

data management and analysis, as well as three invited lectures on different quantitative modeling techniques. These were among the best-attended events at the meeting. In fact, seasoned researchers urged members of the program committee to continue these workshops, which they viewed as a kind of continuing education for researchers. In addition, student members provided very favorable reviews, citing how the workshops supplemented their classes. Clearly, the Program Committee had identified a need in the field to provide both experienced and junior researchers with guides to best practices in quantitative methods. It is worth saying that it is always challenging to keep up with advances in one's field. The incentives for staying current in methods are considerable, however, because newer methods typically enable researchers to test their hypotheses better. Why have we selected *Monographs of the Society for Research in Child Development* for a publication outlet instead of a publishing house? The answer is that monographs is more likely to get into more hands that can and will use it to improve the field.

There is great variability in the quantitative methods training that developmentalists receive through their doctoral programs, housed in departments including anthropology, economics, education, human development, psychology, and sociology. Some program requirements are modest at best, while others are rigorous; further, some universities offer a large array of courses that students may elect to take, while others lack the human resources to do so. Even students motivated to learn quantitative methods need to balance this goal with the goal of learning content knowledge in developmental science; moreover, requirements in qualitative methods, valuable in their own right, may remove a degree of freedom or two from students who want to devote their time to studying quantitative methods. Although there are clearly advantages to learning as much as possible about quantitative methods while a student, all researchers need to keep abreast of evolving quantitative methods. In the 20-plus years since the first two authors have been doctoral students, there have been dramatic advances in methods. In fact, very little information covered in this monograph was available to researchers 25 years ago.

The field in general and the SRCD in particular has demonstrated a commitment to publishing both articles that use advanced statistical methods to address substantive issues and to demonstrate new statistical methods to developmentalists. During the past 25 years, the SRCD and other professional organizations have published seminal work that acquainted developmentalists with newer and better statistical methods. In each case, the authors described, in an accessible manner, methods that were already developed and had been published in quantitative literature. The goal was to make developmentalists aware that these methods existed and to provide them with enough information that they could use those methods in their work. These articles include work by Rubin (1976), detailing then-cutting-edge techniques for addressing problems of missing data; McCall and Appelbaum (1973), demonstrating the multivariate approach to repeated measures analysis as an improved method for repeated measures analysis; Overton (1998) summarizing recent techniques for qualitative data, including Item Response Theory (IRT) scaling models; Raudenbush and Bryk (1986), describing hierarchical linear models as an improved method for repeated measures analysis; McArdle and Epstein (1987), presenting latent growth curves as another method for estimating growth curves; Burchinal and Appelbaum (1991), articulating the role of theories of change in selecting growth curve models; Nagin and Tremblay (2001), presenting growth mixture models as a means to identify groups with different developmental trajectories; Collins and Sayer (2001) and Singer and Willett (2003), summarizing many recent advances in longitudinal data analysis; Baron and Kenny (1986), defining the role of mediation and moderation analyses in testing developmental theories; and NICHD ECCRN and Duncan (2003), for articulating the many issues that can bias conclusions in observational studies and describing some econometric methods to address these issues. Each of these articles has been widely cited, and many changed expectations regarding analysis of developmental data. This is by no means a comprehensive list, but, like these works, our hope is that this monograph will make already developed methods accessible to developmentalists so they can understand and use them in their research.

The need to learn newer methods comes not only from advances in methodology, but also from increasing interdisciplinarity across the sciences, including the social sciences. For decades, developmental researchers have borrowed concepts and procedures from other disciplines, including anthropology, biology, economics, education, and sociology, to name a few, in an effort to understand and explain developmental patterns. Today, there is a widely shared view among researchers that most problems require solutions that involve contributions from across the disciplines. For example, Mansilla (2004) reminds us that "a deep understanding of contemporary life requires an interdisciplinary approach. Such understanding demands that we draw on multiple sources of expertise in order to capture multi-dimensional phenomena, produce complex explanations, or solve intricate problems" (p. 2). A good example in the developmental sciences comes from interdisciplinary work between economists and psychologists on early childhood programs. Economists are bringing newer methods to understand potential selection bias to psychologists, for example instrumental variables analysis, while psychologists are bringing measurement and developmental processes to the attention of economists. Organizations and institutions are beginning to promote interdisciplinary research as a way to foster a holistic approach to understanding a problem or to examining developmental patterns. Increasing interdisciplinary work will likely increase the need to learn new methods.

We selected each of these chapter topics based on our experiences as reviewers, teachers, and researchers, and it is our belief that attention to each topic will advance the field of developmental science considerably. We start at the beginning with chapters on data management and measurement, two neglected topics in methods training despite the fact that every investigation should begin with proper consideration of each. We follow with two important topics for developmental research, missing data and growth modeling. Missing data can plague developmental work because participants sometimes miss one or more assessment points. Growth modeling methods offer researchers a true means to assess change over time as compared with cruder methods like difference scores and residualized change scores. Then comes a discussion of mediation and moderation, two tools that can be used to elucidate developmental processes. Because so much developmental science is nonexperimental, we include a chapter on selection bias that compares five modeling strategies. Proper attention to data management, measurement, missing data, growth modeling (whenever possible), mediation and moderation, and potential selection bias is guaranteed to result in greater precision in inference making. Even when researchers make good decisions about methods, it is critical for them to use good judgment about the practical importance of findings, so we conclude with this important discussion.

Authors were invited to write user-friendly chapters, which we described as how-to guides. Each author begins with an overview of the issue at hand, describes tensions where they exist, provides illustrious examples (especially for formulae), and offers helpful resources, such as citations to websites and programming code. Authors have prepared easy-to-understand introductions to their topics so that researchers will be able to get started. In some cases, getting started may mean having the tools to practice a new technique with existing data; in other cases, it may mean reading suggested references; and in still other cases, it may mean turning to a colleague with a suggestion for a study based on a new method.

In the first chapter, Margaret Burchinal and Eloise Neebe suggest a set of data entry and data management practices that can eliminate much of the error accidentally introduced by typical practices. Whereas high-quality data management practices help to maintain the integrity of data during collection and analysis, poor quality practices often substantially denigrate the quality of the data. The end result is the introduction of considerable error into the data and thus a reduction in power to detect hypothesized effects. Because developmental researchers frequently face the challenge of marginal statistical power due to limited sample sizes, it is essential to avoid introducing this extraneous error during data collection and analysis.

Drawing on practices used in industry and medical clinical trials, the authors provide suggestions for entry and management practices that will improve the quality of data. The authors conclude that although costly, especially in terms of time, the payoff for investing in high-quality entry and management practices is great. To quote an old adage, the longest way is the shortest way.

In the second chapter, Richard Lambert, Lauren Nelson, Denise Brewer, and Margaret Burchinal present traditional psychometric and newer IRT approaches to measurement. Most constructs of interest to developmentalists are somewhat abstract and cannot be directly measured. As a result, the need for high-quality measurement is great. The authors describe two techniques—classical test theory and item response theory—and highlight the strengths and weaknesses of each method. Classical test theory approaches produce instruments in which the reliability and validity of scale scores or total scores are used to index the quality of the instrument. IRT relies on scaling procedures that focus both on the extent to which the instrument measures ability for a population with certain ability levels and provides an estimate of ability for each individual within those populations. The authors advocate the use of IRT scaling methods over classical methods for obtaining information about the technical quality of a scale score. This technique reduces the influence of measurement error on estimates of association between variables and thereby increases the statistical power of inferential procedures.

In the third chapter, Keith Widaman describes methods designed to provide appropriate analyses when some of the data are missing. In most courses on research methods and statistical analysis in social science programs, students learn about analytic techniques using sample data sets that have complete data. Yet, missing data are a constant issue in developmental research and are particularly problematic in longitudinal studies. The author describes various types of missing data and contrasts approaches to imputing missing data. The consequences of ignoring and imputing missing data are illustrated with example analyses. Widaman provides a series of analysis recommendations ranging from examining descriptive statistics to determine the extent of missing data, to conducting a series of analyses to assess the sensitivity of results to different approaches. He concludes by suggesting that researchers investigate new methods for addressing the problem of missing data to insure more accurate, and less biased, estimates of associations between variables.

In the fourth chapter, Margaret Burchinal, Lauren Nelson, and Michele Poe provide an overview of growth curve methods, which model change over time, thereby addressing continuity in development. Methods for analyzing longitudinal data provide researchers with powerful tools for describing patterns of developmental change over time and for identifying predictors of variation in developmental change. A wide variety of analytic methods are readily available, but not all researchers know how or when to use each of these methods. The authors describe and contrast traditional repeated measures approaches such as the univariate and multivariate methods, hierarchical linear models, latent growth curve models, as well as person-centered approaches such as trajectory analysis and latent profile analysis. These five methods are each illustrated using a simulated data set from a child-care intervention study. The authors recommend that researchers carefully consider factors such as whether measurement of the attribute resulted in ignorably missing data, time-structured data, time-varying covariates, and error in predictors and outcomes when selecting a method for analyzing longitudinal data.

In the fifth chapter, Eric Dearing and Lawrence Hamilton summarize contemporary methods to test mediation and moderation. Because some variables amplify, diminish, or qualitatively alter the influences of others, mediation and moderation are fundamental statistical tools for researchers interested in developmental processes. These tools offer developmentalists the means to examine possible mechanisms influencing development (mediation) and how some processes appear to have larger effects in some populations or be amplified or diminished by other processes (moderation). The authors review the current consensus on best statistical practices for examining mediating and moderating processes, provide a primer for those unfamiliar with these practices, and direct readers toward resources that simplify their application. The authors conclude by recommending that the product of the coefficients be used to test mediation effects and that the significance of the interaction term be used to test moderation effects. Further, they suggest that researchers must supplement their tests of moderation with an examination of simple slopes and regions of significance.

In the sixth chapter, Kathleen McCartney, Kristen Bub, and Margaret Burchinal present statistical methods used to address bias due to selection factors. Developmentalists often must rely on observational studies to identify developmental processes because we cannot randomly assign children to treatments, such as poverty. Economists argue that most developmental studies do not provide unbiased estimates of association because of possible selection bias (i.e., causal links with other unmeasured variables that account for the observed association). The authors illustrate newer selection methods with an example: the effect of maternal employment hours on children's math achievement. Four methods are demonstrated: multiple regression with covariates, fixed effects analysis, propensity score analysis, and instrumental variables analysis, and one is discussed, regression discontinuity analysis. The authors advocate comparing findings across models, whenever possible, to determine the robustness of findings.

In the final chapter, Roger Bakeman provides guidelines for data interpretation to reveal the practical importance of findings. Developmentalists must be cognizant of the fact that decisions about children's lives are often influenced by the papers we write. Yet, most of our analytic work focuses on whether there is an association between two variables and does not adequately address the practical importance of these associations. In this chapter, the author illustrates various methods for data screening to identify distributional problems prior to data analysis, provides suggestions for creating tables and figures that optimally present information, and offers an overview of methods for estimating effect sizes. He concludes by reminding researchers that data must be carefully screened, that analysis and description are best kept separate, and that consideration of the presentation and interpretation of results, including a discussion of effect size estimates, are necessary steps when evaluating the practical importance of findings.

We hope this monograph will serve as a guide to best practices in quantitative research methods for developmentalists, both seasoned researchers desiring continued education and newer researchers learning methods afresh. We also hope it will contribute to the long history of work that is useful to developmental researchers. Our main goal has been to bring research to practice with respect to developmental methods and thereby to help researchers increase the quality of their work. As new methods emerge, we hope a new volume will take the place of this one. We conclude by stating the obvious: better methods will result in better research and better research will result in advances in child development.

REFERENCES

Baron, R. M., & Kenny, D. A. (1986). The moderator-mediator variable distinction in social psychological research: Conceptual, strategic, and statistical considerations. *Journal of Personality and Social Psychology*, **51**, 1173–1182.

Burchinal, M., & Appelbaum, M. I. (1991). Estimating individual developmental functions: Methods and their assumptions. *Child Development*, **62**, 23–43.

Collins, L. M. & Sayer, A. (Eds.), (2001). *New methods for the analysis of change*. Washington, DC: American Psychological Association.

Mansilla, V. B. (2004). Assessing student work at disciplinary crossroads. *GoodWork*® *Project Report Series, Number 33*.

McArdle, J. J., & Epstein, D. (1987). Latent growth models within developmental structural equation models. *Child Development*, **58**, 110–133.

McCall, R. B., & Appelbaum, M. I. (1973). Bias in the analysis of repeated-measures designs: Some alternative approaches. *Child Development*, **44**, 401–415.

Nagin, D. S., & Tremblay, R. E. (2001). Analyzing developmental trajectories of distinct but related behaviors: A group-based method. *Psychological Methods*, **6**, 18–34.

NICHD Early Child Care Research Network, & Duncan, G. J. (2003). Modeling the impacts of child care quality on children's preschool cognitive development. *Child Development*, **74**, 1454–1475.

Overton, W. F. (1998). Developmental psychology: Philosophy, concepts, and methodology. In W. Damon & R. Lerner (Eds.), *Handbook of child psychology: Volume 1: Theoretical models of human development* (5th ed., pp. 993–1028). Hoboken, NJ: John Wiley and Sons.

Raudenbush, S., & Bryk, A. S. (1986). A hierarchical model for studying school effects. *Sociology of Education*, **59**, 1–17.

Rubin, D. B. (1976). Inference and missing data. *Biometrika*, **63**, 581–592.

Singer, J. D., & Willett, J. B. (2003). *Applied longitudinal data analysis: Modeling change and event occurrence*. New York, NY: Oxford Press.

I. DATA MANAGEMENT: RECOMMENDED PRACTICES

The purpose of data management is to preserve data integrity between data collection and analysis. Non-optimal data management practices can introduce substantial amounts of error into the data, thereby reducing power to test hypotheses and wasting the project resources devoted to ensuring reliability in data collection. The purpose of this chapter is to suggest data entry and management practices that can eliminate much of this error, provide examples, and demonstrate the essential role of documentation. We believe that implementation of these data management and documentation practices can greatly enhance the quality of developmental research.

Data management entails entering, cleaning, scoring, and processing data. High-quality practices focus on reducing the amount of error added at any of these stages. Data entry practices include independent data entry and checks against the original forms when discrepancies are detected. Data cleaning should include range checks for items to ensure values for all items and scale scores are valid and to provide computer scoring of all instruments. Data processing should include consistency checks within and across data sets and the creation of new versions of data sets as identified errors in the data are corrected. All of these practices are described in more detail as follows.

The need for such practices was illustrated by one project at our research institute. The project coordinator trained graduate and post-doctoral students to administer developmental tests. All students met strict training criteria before beginning data collection but had no training in scoring and entering the data. They then administered and scored the tests, and entered the summary scores into a computer file. Several years into the project, analyses yielded odd patterns of gains and losses. The data management and analysis center was asked to audit the data by checking the database against the items in the original test forms. Across five tests for each of 80 children, 55% of the test scores in the data set were incorrect and 20% had serious errors that resulted in changes of more than five points on standard scores. The problems included incorrect computation of standard scores due to entering the wrong dates or computing the number of items passed incorrectly, incorrectly entering identification (ID) values thereby assigning developmental scores to the wrong individual, and incorrect entry of scores into the database.

The error introduced during data processing in this example is not usual. We have detected 5–10% error rates linked to data management when data are entered only once and error rates of over 10% when research assistants score and enter developmental test data in projects that depended on their lab for data collection and scoring before turning to our data center for data entry and processing. Implementation of quality practices can eliminate almost all of these errors.

Funding agencies now recognize the need for high-quality data management. The National Institutes of Health (NIH) acknowledged the need for high standards for data management by requiring professional data managers for large NIH-funded projects. NIH has argued that professional data centers are needed because "even in natural history studies, such infrastructure can only enhance the quality of and access to the research by ensuring that data are collected as required by the protocol and are stored in a way that allows access to the information without dependence on any individual clinical researcher" (National Institutes of Health, 2000).

Many of the current quality assurance practices were developed for clinical trials designed to evaluate the effectiveness of new medical treatments. These criteria require that, before data collection, programmers design databases and write programs for data entry and processing. These programs check that data are consistent and within valid ranges at every stage of data management and analysis. Each step in collecting, entering, scoring, and analyzing the data is completely documented so that it is possible to identify who was responsible for, and what was done at, each stage of data collection, entry, and processing. This procedure results in data that are very accurate (often less than 0.5% error added during data management) and well documented, but it can be very expensive to implement. We believe there is an affordable compromise that will increase data integrity. Such recommended practices are described the next sections (U.S. Food and Drug Administration, 1998, 2005).

RECOMMENDED STANDARD PRACTICES

Data management should be a consideration from the design of the protocol until the project ends and the data are archived. Standard data management practices are listed and briefly defined in Table 1. Adopting

TABLE 1

STANDARD DATA MANAGEMENT PRACTICES

Database design
Tracking system
Independent double entry of data
Range and validity checking for all data
Psychometric analyses of summary scores
Thorough documentation

some or all of these practices should increase the integrity of data during data keying and processing.

Before Data Collection

The structure and contents of the database should be designed and a tracking system should be created before data collection. The database consists of all files containing data, programs, or documents associated with a given project. Designing the database involves multiple steps.

Step one is determining the ID system. A consistent and comprehensive ID system should be conceived that uniquely identifies each record. This entails creating a unique ID system for each participating target individual in all studies, for time in longitudinal studies, and for classrooms and schools in studies in which multiple children attend the same class or for family members in studies in which multiple family members are tracked over time. These IDs should provide unique identification across nested factors such as time, family members, or schools. For example, it is often advisable in longitudinal studies of families to have a separate ID for each man who lives with the mother or for each person who serves as the primary caregiver for a child to capture changes in who served as parents to the target child. Similarly, in longitudinal studies of children in classrooms you need a separate ID for teacher and classroom so that you can determine when classroom data are collected with different teachers. IDs must be unique within category (e.g., child, family member, school) and should be easy to enter and check.

Step two is designing a master file. The master file contains all of the important information that can be used across multiple instruments such as gender and birth date. It is important to ensure that relevant IDs are entered on all forms before data collection along with built-in checks such as birth date and assessment data. Then values for ID, gender, and birth date in the master file can be checked against the values of ID, gender, and birth date on forms as they are entered. If discrepancies exist, the programmer can flag the incorrect ID and ask the data collectors to provide a correct ID.

11

TABLE 2

EXAMPLE DIRECTORY STRUCTURE FOR PROJECT
DATA MANAGEMENT AND ANALYSIS

XYZ study
  Analysis
    SRCD 05
      Programs
      Documentation
    Risk paper
      Programs
      Documentation
  Bayley
    Programs
    Data
    Documentation
    Print
  CESD
    Programs
    Data
    Documentation
    Print

Indeed, incorrect entry of IDs is one of the most common errors made by data collectors.

Step three involves designing the database. The structure of the database should reflect the various types of data and the timing or waves of data collection. We suggest a separate directory for each instrument or form collected, with separate subdirectories for programs, data sets, and documentation (see Table 2 for a hypothetical example). In this example, there is a directory for all analysis files, with separate subdirectories for analyses specific to a given presentation or paper. The two analysis subdirectories contain all programs and memos or other forms of documentation. In addition, there is a directory for each instrument. The program directory contains all programs used to enter, score, and update the data sets. The data directory contains the data files. The documentation directory contains all communication with the project staff regarding the data collected on that instrument such as lists of errors in the data and instructions on how to correct those errors. The print directory contains copies of the output from all programs used to process the data. The information in these four directories should ensure that all data files can be traced accurately from data collection through data analysis to published paper.

Step four entails planning data entry and processing. Specific quality assurance practices will vary depending on whether data are collected on paper forms or electronically, but the fundamental principles exist regardless of the mode of data collection. Electronic data collection can include computer-assisted personal interviews (CAPI) as well as data collected through other machines ranging from palm pilots to comprehensive brain scans such as MRIs. With electronic data collection, you must select a reliable transfer of the data from the machine used for data collection into the project database (e.g., File Transfer Programs or FTP to a secure server). With paper data collection, plans for data keying must be developed as discussed in more detail as follows. Regardless of whether the data are collected electronically or on paper, data entry plans should ensure that questionable values are identified during data entry and either resolved or flagged for later examination. The project staff should provide a list of acceptable values (i.e., valid ranges) for each datum and a list of fields that are required for each form (e.g., subject ID, instrument identifier, date of data collection, and essential data from that instrument). This information should be used to check as data are collected electronically or keyed. All values outside these ranges should be flagged for further inspection and likely correction.

The best method for data keying of data collected on paper forms is independent data entry by two individuals, followed by comparisons of the two files. If discrepancies occur, the keyed values can be compared with the paper form. A unique identifier should be used for each instrument to ensure that data can be processed into the correct database and corrections can be applied to those data files.

The next part of planning the data management system is developing a structure for creating the data sets that will organize the data in a logical manner. This involves creating conventions for naming variable, writing labels for all variables, and setting up checks for inconsistencies and other possible errors. Systematic naming of variables can convey information about the instrument used to collect the data, the informant, timing of data collection, and whether the variable was directly assessed (e.g., an item) or computed from other scores. Variables should be unique across all data sets. If consistent naming conventions are used, then it is easier to ascertain the exact meaning of each variable. A label should be attached to each variable that succinctly describes the instrument, time of data collection, and whether the variable is a single item or a summary score. Part of developing the overall structure is identifying, whether responses are consistent within data sets, relative to the master file, and relative to missing values elsewhere in the data sets.

The final step before data collection involves setting up a tracking system that allows the project coordinator and programmers to follow the progress (or lack thereof) in data collection. The purpose is to document the status of data collection and processing by tracking data collection for each subject, for each instrument within a panel, and for each instrument across panels. This system documents the extent to which each participant is

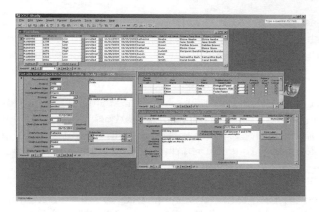

FIGURE 1.—Examples from the tracking system for a longitudinal project.

Form Acronym	Forms Received	Forms Tracked	Keying Completed	Reconciled	Version	Error Detection	Data/Errors sent to project	Errors/Verification returned to FPG	Corrs. Completed	Comments
BSI	5/15/00 5/17/00 5/25/00 5/31/00	5/17/00 5/24/00 5/25/00 5/31/00	6/15/00	6/19/00	01	1/10/01	1/16/01 ER V1,2,3,4	3/9/01	3/12/01	A few corrections in V01A.
	7/24/00	7/26/00	7/31/00	8/7/00	02	1/10/01	1/16/01 ER V1,2,3,4	3/9/01	3/12/01	9 forms
	6/1/01	7/1/01	8/01	8/20/01	08	9/17/01	10/3/01	12/14/01	12/21/01	
	11/1/01	11/1/01	12/01	1/9/02	09	1/16/02	3/12/02			Scored
	2/13/02	2/13/02	4/02	5/1/02	10	5/1/02	5/13/02	9/02	9/11/02	V10A SCORED
	6/1/02	6/1/02	7/15/02	7/24/02	11	7/24/02	9/24/02			SCORED
	9/6/02	9/02	9/02	10/2/02	12	No errors	10/3/02	NA	NA	V12A SCORED
	10/02	10/02	12/02	1/7/03	13	5/19/03	6/5/03			V13A SCORED
	4/2003	4/2003	5/2003	5/12/03	14	5/19/03	6/5/03		6/9/03	V14A, V14B SCORED
	Sum 03	Sum 03	10/03	11/3/03	15	11/12/03	11/13/03	11/20/03	11/24/03	GA corrs done
	Fall 03	Fall 03	1/04	2/5/04	16	2/20/04	2/24/04	4/04	4/04	

FIGURE 2.—Example data status report from a tracking system.

scheduled and complete data are collected for each individual. Figure 1 shows an example of pages from a tracking system used in a longitudinal project and Figure 2 shows a report generated from this system showing the status of data collection. In addition to documenting how the data were collected, tracking systems should also document which data should be missing and why. A tracking system is useful for research coordinators to monitor progress of data collection as well as for programmers. Tracking system can vary from simple tables to complex multi-page systems.

14

Data Processing During Data Collection

Careful attention to quality assurance during data keying and processing will reduce the likelihood of introducing error. These quality assurance practices include creating a series of permanent data sets and using version numbers to identify the most recent updates. The first permanent data set is created when the data are keyed or transferred electronically. Subsequent permanent data sets are as occurs when new data are added or changes are made to the data in that data set and these new data sets are assigned names that indicate that they are revisions of the previous data set.

The first step in data processing involves creating the data set in the research database. After data are keyed and discrepancies resolved or data are transferred electronically, a permanent data set is created within the database that adheres to the principle and decisions made during the planning stage. All data must have the same ID variables as used in the other data sets in the database. Often identifying information must be recoded when data are transferred from clinical settings so that ID information in those data sets matches the ID information in the rest of the database. Next, the programmer should make sure that there is the correct number of records for each individual. The programmer needs to flag the data for an individual if the data set includes too many records or too few records for that person. For example, further investigation is needed if the project staff indicates that data were collected on 10 different people and there should be one record per person, but the data set includes data on nine individuals with one record for eight people and two records for one person. In this case, the programmer issues an error report to the staff that indicates that no data was received for one person who should have been in the data set, but that two records were received for another person. The project staff would be asked to check the printout of the data against the original data forms to determine what changes are needed.

At this time all fields should be checked to make sure that values are acceptable values as stipulated by the research staff and are internally consistent. The first check involves determining whether the ID value is consistent with internal checks involving variables such as date of birth or gender. The programmer can check whether the gender or birth date for each individual in the new data set match the gender and birth date for the individual with that ID in a master file. An error report is issued whenever discrepancies are found so that project staff can correct the ID if necessary. This type of checking is especially important because typing ID values incorrectly is one of the most common errors by research staff. In addition, the programmer should check whether fields are within acceptable ranges and whether missing values exist for variables that are supposed to have complete data.

15

```
***check for duplicates on key variables;
data _null_;
set lib.&form.v&ver;
by id tgrade; file print;
if first.tgrade ne last.tgrade or not first.tgrade then
put / "Duplicate: " id= tgrade=; run;

***check data internally and against master file;
%macro checkit(whr,t);
data _null_;
merge lib.&form.v&ver(in=ins)
dem.&demdat(in=ind keep=id birthdt sex gk g1-g9 initial1 initial2 initial3);
by id; if ins;

***check for bad id;
if not ind then put / "Check for invalid id: " id= tgrade= agrade=;

***include customized file to check key variables, id agrade tgrade date;
%include "l:\ome\checks2003_2004V1.txt";

***check dob; if dob ne birthdt than put / "Check dob: " id= tgrade= dob= birthdt=;

***check variable range;
array hsq (14) hspq_a1-hspq_a14;
do i = 1 to 14;
            if hsq{i} not in (1,2,3,4,5) then put / "Answer out of range (1 - 5):
            " id= agrade= tgrade= date= hsq{i}=;
      end;
```

FIGURE 3.—SAS code for checking data.

The programmer issues error reports whenever he or she determines there is likely a problem with the data. Figure 3 shows a part of a SAS program that runs a series of checks for more than record per individual, consistency of ID and other information relative to master file, and for invalid or questionable values for the fields in the inputed data. An error message is written to a report when any of those problems are detected. Figure 4 provides an example generated by the SAS code in Figure 3. As you can see, the programmer provides information about whose data are questionable and what the problem was and then requests that the project staff provide a correction. The form will show what changes were made and when; after the project staff member responds to each item, the form will indicate whether a change was made on the original data collection form as a consequence of the detected error and, if so, the reason for the correction. The research staff member should initial and date each requested change. This report becomes part of the documentation for the project so that the staff can always tell why data in the data set may differ from data on the paper form or the inputted data sets.

XYZ Study
BSI Brief Symptom Inventory
Possible Errors - Version: 06

Initials of Reviewer to Approve the Error Correction Form Changes: ____ Date: ___

ID year batch variable message old_value new_value comment

12345 2004-2005 6 BSI01 Value is Missing ____

12345 2004-2005 6 BSI05 Invalid value 10 ____

12345 2004-2005 6 BSI11 Value is Missing . ____

l:\XYZStudy\bsi\pgm\bsi_32.sas

FIGURE 4.—Example of an error report generated by checking program.

Several quality assurance practices also should be considered when updating or changing data sets. Data sets must be updated whenever corrections are made or new data are added. Corrections are usually made based on the responses from the research staff to reports of possible errors detected during range and validity checks. The programmer writes a program that makes those corrections, runs validity checks on the changes, and creates a new version of the data set. Similarly, the programmer writes a program to merge old and new data, runs validity checks on the new data, and creates a new version of the data set. For example, the first version of a data set with language scores is created with the first data are keyed or electronically uploaded and is called Lang01. If keying the data identified errors, then the programmer asks the research team to resolve the problems. He or she then writes a program that reads the Lang01 data set, makes the corrections specified by the research staff, runs validity checks on the changed data, and names the resulting data set Lang02. Then if new data is keyed or uploaded, the programmer merges the old and new data, runs validity checks on the new data, and creates a new data set Lang03. At each stage the new data are checked for invalid, questionable, or inconsistent data at each stage of data processing. In addition, at each stage, a new version of the data set is created so that old versions are not destroyed and can be retrieved if needed. Finally, the programmer must document all changes and decisions made during data processing.

Scoring Data During Data Processing

Programmers can greatly increase the quality of the data by scoring assessments with computer programs instead of having research assistants score them. The scoring instructions should be provided to the programmer by the research staff. Ideally, the programmer receives a copy of the manual for developmental assessments or other measures that require complicated scoring algorithms. The programmer then runs checks on the ID values, dates, and items to make sure that the instrument was administered correctly. For example, the programmer will check to make sure the ID appears correct using procedures described above. He or she will then check to make sure that the administration date and birth date are correct if standardized scores are to be computed. The basal and ceiling rules will be checked and violations flagged. Ideally, scoring programs can be purchased from or donated by the instrument developers (or their corporate representatives) for the most complicated measures such as standardized cognitive and achievement tests and should be used to prevent errors. We have found that even experienced staff members are prone to making substantive errors when asked to score such data by hand.

Analysis Data Sets

Permanent data sets for specific analyses should be created only when data are completely entered, cleaned, and frozen. It is often tempting to create an "analysis" data set when you are ready to work on a paper, and to include all of the data—typically from multiple data sets—in one analysis data set to make it easier to run the analyses. The problem with the solution is that the programmer may be making correction to or adding new data to the project data sets, but is unlikely to update each of these analysis data sets. Thus, using the analysis data set can result in analyses of data that either do not include all possible subjects or do not reflect corrections of values identified as problematic.

Instead, we recommend that all manipulations needed to create your analysis data set be represented in a single program. This program is run each time you conduct analysis. There are several advantages to using a single program to pull together all of the data, recode data, and delete ineligible cases rather than using an analysis data set. First, any updates to the data sets will be maintained in analysis because your program can read in the most recent version of every data set and thus use all new data in your analysis. Second, this program will provide complete documentation about all decisions made regarding whom to include in analyses, recoding variables, and creation of summary variables.

Documentation

Creation of comprehensive documentation for a project is one of the most valuable roles that professional data management personnel provide for a research team. As stated in NIH and FDA guidelines, professional data management should yield data in which all changes and scoring decisions are apparent at every stage of the research, from data collection through analysis. Documentation is created to describe each step of the process and should be available both electronically and in print form.

Data set management decisions should be documented electronically both in the data sets and as separate files within the database. All variables should be labeled in each data set in a manner that conveys information even after data sets are merged. For example, a label of "summary score" is not useful outside the data set for that instrument, whereas a label "PPVT-III Dev Quotient" is useful after data from multiple instruments are merged together. Each label should succinctly state which instrument generated the data, the time of data collection if relevant, and a brief description of the measure. To take the example further, the label "PK fall PPVT-III Dev Quotient" would be most effective if data from separate waves of data collection are stored in different data sets. For items, it is nice to number them as they are numbered in the instrument (e.g., "PK fall, PPVT-III item 1").

Titles or footnotes can provide another form of documentation. We add the full name of each program as a footnote to all programs. The title for each program should include the project, date, and a brief description of the purpose of the program. We have found these practices to be invaluable, especially with longitudinal projects, when investigators bring us an old print or program and ask us to duplicate whatever was done in that program.

Codebooks or annotated forms should be created to describe each instrument, to map variable names onto the data collected, and document decisions made during data keying and processing. Figure 5 shows an example of an annotated form. This is the form used for data collection with variable names superimposed onto the form. Looking at this annotated form, it is possible to determine for each variable exactly what question was asked and what responses were possible. Included at the bottom of the form are instructions for creating all summary variables. In this project, we asked the staff to provide information about each instrument such as the name, the citation, a brief description, and scoring information. We inserted this information on the form used for data collection and stored in a documentation directory. These codebooks have been invaluable for quick access to both the data collection forms and information about the instrument.

In addition to electronic documentation, printed documentation is valuable. In our own case we have a notebook or set of notebooks for each project. Ideally, this notebook includes a copy of the proposal or some other description of the project, copies of all versions of all data collection instruments and scoring instructions for each, a codebook for each instrument or data set, and a copy of all communications including error reports and their responses. These notebooks provide a complete set of documentation for the project.

Psychometric Analysis of Summary Variables

The programmer can build the computation of reliability and validity measures into the planning and implementation of the research database

FAMILY LIFE PROJECT
INSTRUMENT DOCUMENTATION
Name of Instrument / Citation: Role Overload Scale (adapted from)

Reilly, M.D. (1982). Working wives and convenience consumption. *Journal of Consumer Research, 8,* 407-418.

INVESTIGATOR RESPONSIBLE FOR MEASURE: Crouter

RELEVANT RESEARCH

Crouter, Ann C., Bumpus, Matthew F., Head, Melissa R., & McHale, Susan M. (2001). Implications of overwork and overload for the quality of men's family relationships. *Journal of Marriage and Family, 63* (2), 404-417.

This is a study on the implications of men's work and the quality of their family relationships. The sample was 190 dual-earner working middle class families. During phase one of this study, fathers completed the Reilly's Role Overload Scale. Men's feelings of role overload were a more important predictor of the quality of the marriage than long hours of work. However, men's relationship with firstborn and secondborn adolescent offspring was associated with the combination of overload and long hours of work.

Purpose:

The Role Overload Scale was originally developed by Reilly in 1982. It was based on earlier work by House and Rizzo in 1972. The scale measures the respondent's sense that there is too much to do and not enough time to do it. The current study uses a modified, 6-item version of the original 13-item measure. Each question is answered on a 5-point Likert Scale, ranging from *strongly agree* to *strongly disagree*. The scale is completed by the primary and secondary caregivers at the 6-Month Home Visit A.

Time: Under 5 Minutes

Number of items: There are 6 questions.

Training and Administration: The scale is self-administered

CURRENT USE:

Participant Age: Mothers/primary caregivers and fathers/secondary caregivers at the 6-month home interview.

Administration: Administered via computer using Blaise software. The Household Composition Questionnaire is read to the primary caregiver by the home visitor.

Where Administered: In home

Special Circumstances of Administration: None

Computer Scored: Yes

Reliability: Both mothers and fathers competed the 13-item role overload scale during Phase 1 of the study described in Crouter et al. (1999). Cronbach's alphas were .89 for mothers ($M = 46.9$; $SD = 9.0$) and .92 for fathers ($M = 43.6$; $SD = 10.5$).

FIGURE 5.—Example of an annotated form used for project documentation.

Validity: In Crouter et al. (1999) fathers' reports of greater feelings of role overload were significantly associated with increased feelings of work pressure ($r = .37$, $p < .001$). Similarly, mothers' reports of greater feelings of role overload were significantly associated with increased feelings of work pressure ($r = .38$, $p < .001$)

Scoring: Average and mean the items: All items should be reverse scored prior to taking sum or mean, such that higher scores reflect greater feelings of role overload.

ROv_Sm = Role Overload Scale Total Sum of all reverse scored items 1 to 6, pro-rating the sum if one of the six items is missing, and calculating the score only if at least 5 items are non-missing.

ROv_Mn = Role Overload Scale Total Mean of all reverse scored items 1 to 6. Score is calculated only if there are at least 5 responses with values other than N/A, don't know or refuse.

Missing Data Procedures: At least 5 of the 6 items are required to be non-missing to score.

Modifications: Only 6 of the original 13 items are used in the current version of the scale.

ROLE OVERLOAD

		Strongly Agree	Mildly Agree	Neither Agree or Disagree	Mildly Disagree	Strongly Disagree
1.	**ROv1** There are too many demands on my time.	1	2	3	4	5
2.	**ROv2** I need more hours in the day to do all the things which are expected of me.	1	2	3	4	5
3.	**ROv3** I can't ever seem to get caught up.	1	2	3	4	5
4.	**ROv4** I don't ever seem to have any time for myself.	1	2	3	4	5
5.	**ROv5** Sometimes I feel as if there are not enough hours in the day.	1	2	3	4	5
6.	**ROv6** I seem to have to over-extend myself in order to be able to finish everything I have to do.	1	2	3	4	5

FIGURE 5.—Continued.

management system. Measures of internal consistency can be computed easily during the final data processing of an instrument when research staff members have provided scoring information. Similarly, validity checks such as correlations can be computed. This information can then be included in the codebook and easily cited when papers are being written.

Maintaining Confidentiality

Confidentiality must be maintained during data entry and processing as in every other stage of research. All personal identifying information should be removed from forms before data entry and should not be stored in project data sets. Materials or data sets with identifying information such as name, social security number, or birth dates should be stored in locked files. Data sets with such information should not be stored on networks and should be password protected if stored on any computer.

Data Security

The data should be securely stored and backed up regularly. Access to a project directory should be limited to individuals who work on that project. Directories can be password protected or be given access rights based on user ID. Recommended practice is to conduct nightly backups that include all files that changed during the day and weekly backups of all files. It is essential that a regular backup schedule be established, and that a copy of recent backups be stored off site as well as on site.

CONCLUSIONS

Sound data management practices are needed to ensure the integrity of research data. While high-quality practices require that programmers receive specific training in data management practices and be allowed sufficient time to implement those practices, the potential payoff is large. Developmental researchers often face the challenge of marginal statistical power because of small to moderate sample sizes. Consequently, assuring adequate power to test hypotheses makes it essential to avoid introducing extraneous error during data collection and analysis. The practices described here can help to maintain data integrity while providing the research project with comprehensive documentation of how the project was implemented, what each variable means, and exactly how it was scored. Such documentation often is one of the most valuable contributions of the data management and analysis unit, especially with longitudinal projects.

ACKNOWLEDGMENTS

We would like to thank Lynne Vernon-Feagans and Joanne Roberts for allowing us to use examples from the data management for their projects and the many investigators for whom we have provided data management over the past 25 years.

REFERENCES

National Institutes of Health. (2000). *Standards for clinical research within NIH Intramural Research Program*. http://www.cc.nih.gov/ccc/clinicalresearch/standards1.html

U.S. Food and Drug Administration. (1998). *Computerized systems used in clinical trial*. http://www.fda.gov/ora/compliance_ref/bimo/ffinalcct.htm#_Toc444571269.

U.S. Food and Drug Administration. (2005). *Guidances and information sheets on good clinical practice in FDA-regulated clinical trials*. http://www.fda.gov/oc/gcp/guidance.html

II. MEASUREMENT ISSUES AND PSYCHOMETRIC METHODS IN DEVELOPMENTAL RESEARCH

Measurement, in its most basic form, is the process of assigning quantitative values to objects or events according to a set of rules (Stevens, 1948). This process invokes multiple issues. Measuring a construct of interest (e.g., social skills, peer acceptance) requires careful definition of the underlying construct, creation of sensitive instruments for accessing that construct, and reasonable rules for scoring those instruments to produce summary scores. The topic of measurement is broad; we cannot cover the entire field (see Embretson & Reise, 2000, or Wilson, 2005, for a more detailed introduction). The purpose of this chapter is to discuss the steps involved in constructing assessment instruments, describe two measurement models or approaches for scoring them (i.e., classical test theory [CTT] and item response theory [IRT]), and demonstrate these two approaches with an example from our research.

Most constructs of interest to developmentalists are somewhat abstract and cannot be directly measured. For example, although we can measure height exactly, we have to measure constructs such as intelligence or social skills in relativistic ways. That is, we cannot derive a paradigm that will yield an index on a ratio scale that provides isomorphic measurement of those constructs. Accordingly, developmentalists have emphasized the need for high-quality measurement. The basic properties that the information yielded by an instrument must possess to be considered useful to developmentalists have been codified into a set of rules called the Standards for Educational and Psychological Measurement (Standards) (American Educational Research Association [AERA], American Psychological Association [APA], and the National Council on Measurement in Education [NCME], 1999).

RULES AS EMBODIED BY THE STANDARDS

The Standards for Educational and Psychological Measurement (American Educational Research Association [AERA] et al., 1999) codify the criteria by which instruments and instrument development work can be judged. The standards provide guidelines for establishing validity evidence based on test content, response processes, internal structure, relationships to the information provided by other measures, and the consequences of using the measure (Wilson, 2005). They also serve as a useful outline for test users and researchers trying to select measures that have demonstrated acceptable technical merit. Selected standards that have particular relevance to developmental research are reviewed as follows, but the reader is referred to the standards for an exhaustive treatment of this topic.

The standards emphasize that the validity of an instrument lies in determining the ability of that instrument to provide the intended information for the intended population. In particular, it is important to ensure that the purpose of the test is consistent with its intended use (e.g., clinical evaluation, screening, or research). Although it has become an unfortunately common practice to use the same instrument for multiple purposes, no measure can successfully sustain numerous demands on the information it provides unless the multiple purposes have been considered during development and validation (Standard 15.1, AERA et al., 1999). In addition, the standards remind us that multiple sources of information are always better for interpretation and decision making than any single measure (Standard 12.18, AERA et al., 1999).

Two of the standards (Standards 2.11 and 2.12) address the generally held principle that the consistency of children's responses to test stimuli, and therefore the reliability, tends to increase with age and across diverse groups. Accordingly, reliability evidence and standard errors of measurement should be reported separately for each age, grade level, or subgroup for which a test is intended. Reliability estimates based on scores from combined age groups or developmental levels are likely to be spuriously high. The younger the age of the children for whom a measure is intended, the narrower the age range of the subgroups must be to estimate reliability.

Standards 7.1, 7.2, and 7.3 urge test makers and users to remain culturally sensitive by attending to potential sources of systematic subgroup (e.g., ethnicity or economic) differences across test scores, sources of measurement error, the factor structure of the test score information, and the strength of the validity evidence for the test scores. Whenever credible evidence of such differences exists, validity information should be collected and reported at the level of the subgroup. For example, questionnaires developed with well-educated middle-class parents need to be validated independently for use with low-income parents with substantially less education. Furthermore, test

25

developers and users are urged to make all reasonable efforts to eliminate influences related to test design, content, and format that may result in test scores that are biased with respect to subgroup membership.

PHASES OF INSTRUMENT DEVELOPMENT

Instrument development involves at least four separate processes (Nunnally & Bernstein, 1994; Wilson, 2005), including construct definition, item construction, scoring strategy specification, and the application of a measurement model. These processes are linked by a set of assumptions, namely that the instrument items provide indicators of a latent construct or attribute being measured and that the scoring system can use this information to create a single or small number of summary scores reflecting the amount of the attribute an individual possesses. The scoring and measurement models are used to create scale scores, which then guide the interpretation and use of test scores in relation to inferences about the respondent.

In general, the same processes should guide instrument development for instruments of all types (e.g., tests directly administered to children, questionnaires, interviews, or rating systems or coding schemes for observations). In each case, construct definition, item construction, scoring strategy specification, and the application of a measurement model are necessary and important steps. A researcher interested in creating an instrument from the definition of a construct must select the mode of measurement (e.g., test, questionnaire, interview, observation), as well as the indicators of the beliefs or behaviors thought to define the construct. These indicators include items in questionnaires or tests, questions in interviews, and either ratings or frequency counts of behaviors in observations. It is important to keep in mind that the value of the instrument being developed depends on the extent to which it successfully taps a given construct.

Following a discussion of the steps used when constructing an instrument, this chapter presents and contrasts the common statistical procedures used within the framework of classical test theory (CTT) to those available within the modern psychometric test theory, item response theory (IRT).

STEPS USED IN CONSTRUCTING USEFUL MEASURES

Construct Definition

The first phase of instrument development, construct definition, includes the following tasks: defining the construct or attribute, establishing the need for the new measure, defining the target population, and defining the purpose and intended uses of the measure (Wilson, 2005). These tasks require the unique blend of a rich theoretical foundation, an informed sense of the gaps in the existing battery of tools, and a sensitivity to the practical constraints involved with assessing the target population. Clearly conceptualizing the construct and its manifestation in beliefs or behaviors is the single most important step in this process (Lord & Novick, 1968). After the construct is defined conceptually, then identification of the target population and the intended uses of the instrument guide the measurement process. A survey of existing instruments is needed to determine whether a new instrument is needed to measure the construct for your intended purpose in your population of interest. Instrument development is difficult and time consuming, and obviously should not be undertaken if adequate instruments already exist.

The intended use of the instrument (clinical decision, screening, research) should affect the measurement process (Wilson, 2005). For example, an instrument used to make a clinical decision must be accurate at the individual level for the intended population, requiring substantially more rigor in development. Instruments used solely for research likely do not need to have the same accuracy in measuring each individual as clinical and screening tools require, but should provide sufficient accuracy to have reasonable power in research studies. For example, a screening tool may need to be lengthy to identify individuals with the condition of interest. In contrast, a researcher may prefer to risk over-identifying the condition in favor of a having a shorter instrument. The burden is also on the developer to communicate clearly to test users the purposes for which the test has been developed and validated. As the impact of the accountability policy climate reaches into settings of care for young children, more and more measures are being applied beyond their intended purposes. Common examples of uses for which measures often were not intended include aggregation and high stakes evaluative inferences, creating additional demands and stressors for practitioners (Lambert, Abbott-Shim, & Sibley, 2006).

Many measures are used by both researchers and practitioners and thus have dual purposes. Test developers and researchers can benefit greatly by becoming familiar with the sets of rules that developmental theorists and practitioner organizations have outlined to guide both the development and use of measurement tools. For example, high-quality assessment has historically been a critical aspect of early childhood research and education (ECE) (Greenspan, Meisels, Barnard, Barrera, Berman, & Bricker, 1994; Pretti-Frontczak, Kowalksi, & Brown, 2002). ECE experts define assessment as the process of gathering information to make decisions about children (Bredekamp & Copple, 1997; McLean, Wolery, & Bailey, 2004; NAEYC, 2003). However, assessment is a broad term that encompasses several purposes for gathering information about children: screening to identify those at-risk for having special needs; diagnostic evaluation of children; monitoring the developmental progress of children to inform instruction, classroom practices, and families; and program evaluation and teacher development (NAEYC, 2003).

Item Construction

The next phase of the development process, item construction, includes the following tasks: outlining the content domain, writing items, piloting items, and revising items (Wilson, 2005). The process of outlining the content domain can be clarified by using mapping techniques, which provide blueprints for item construction. The construct map technique can be used to cross-tabulate targeted levels of mastery, developmental stages, or even item complexity or format, by the key components of the construct (Wilson, 2005). This cross-tabulation creates cells that guide item construction and help ensure that the entire domain is represented by items in proper proportion to the relative importance of their content given the theory that supports the construct. For example, the developer of a test to measure approaches to learning for 4-, 5-, and 6-year-olds might view competence motivation, persistence, attitudes about learning, and cognitive flexibility as dimensions that need to be assessed (e.g., McDermott, Green, Frances, & Stott, 2000). They could create a table in which these dimensions define the columns and the designated ages define the rows. The developer would then enter in the cells the behaviors or beliefs they thought should be displayed among children of that age who were exhibiting that dimension of approaches to learning. Ideally, the table would be used to write a number of items for each cell. The goal is to write at least twice as many items as required given the targeted test length.

These steps rely heavily on theory and expert opinion and are therefore independent of the statistical models that will eventually be used to make inferences from the test scores (Wilson, 2005). It is typical to calculate simple descriptive statistics using pilot data to get a rough estimate of item difficulty and performance. Pilot subjects are often asked to report their understanding of items and to report anything they found to be ambiguous about or missing from the pilot item pool. Items are then revised and retested accordingly. If pilot samples of sufficient size are available, more sophisticated statistical models, discussed later in this chapter, can be applied during this stage to inform the item revision process.

An important step in creating items is determining their measurement level (Stevens, 1948). Items can provide nominal, ordinal, interval, or ratio-level measurement. Nominal items indicate categories, but the categories are not ordered. Responses to ordinal items are ordered categories (e.g.,

Likert-type scales). Responses to interval and ratio-level items should be continuous, with equal intervals. The ratio-level item has an absolute zero that indicates complete absence of the attribute.

How the items are scored depends on whether they are developed using CTT or IRT, but the use of results from the instrument requires special attention. These two approaches are discussed below. Once a scoring system is developed, attention should shift to examining how useful the instrument is and providing clear documentation regarding the instrument and its development. Special attention should be paid to identifying populations for which the test can be used successfully and appropriately and how information from the instrument can be communicated (i.e., attending to cultural sensitivity).

CTT

Psychometric methods such as CTT have been used for the past 50 to 75 years as a means to develop instruments and assess their value (Nunnally & Bernstein, 1994). The instruments, typically questionnaires or educational tests, are developed under CTT using factor analysis (Lord & Novick, 1968). A pool of items or indicators is generated, with the belief that multiple items are measuring the same attribute in slightly different ways. A larger pool of items results in better measurement because more information is gathered about each person upon each repeated administration. Once the pool of items is identified, factor analysis is used to determine the extent to which the items measure a single or multiple dimensions (i.e., latent constructs). A summary score is computed to represent each latent construct as the sum of the items identified as measuring a given dimension. The summary score is computed as either an unweighted or weighted sum of the items defining that unidimensional latent construct. The item mean score and the correlation between an item and the sum of the items for a scale are used to identify items to retain in the scale (Lord & Novick, 1968). Items with high correlations with the total score and with mean scores in the middle of the possible distribution of response are selected. Ideally this process is repeated several times until the optimal set of items based on their mean scores and correlations with the total score are identified and retained for each latent construct measured by the instrument.

The summary scores for each scale are often transformed into norm-referenced scale scores (Nunnally & Bernstein, 1994). That is, after the final set of items is determined, the instrument is administered to a large, hopefully representative sample of children with similar characteristics to the population for whom the measure is intended. This "norming" sample is stratified by age or grade and, perhaps, gender. Within-sample standardized scores are computed for each stratum, and the scores typically have a mean of 50 and standard deviation of 10 (e.g., t-scores for measures of social skills) or a mean of 100 and standard deviation of 15 (e.g., scaled scores for educational or cognitive tests). These standardized scores are then used to create cross-tabulations of the raw and standardized scores within each stratum, and those tables are used to assign standard scores when the instrument is used for children not in the norming population. Other scaled scores include age-standardized scores, grade equivalent scores, normalized t-scores, and stanines—and each is based on the distribution of the raw scores within the strata of norming sample. All of these scaling techniques result in scores that are measures of relative position within the norming sample or subgroup norming sample, and as such are completely dependent upon the composition of the norming samples.

Under CTT, the quality of an instrument is assessed based on the extent to which the summary score yields the same score when individuals with the same attributes are assessed (i.e., reliability) as well as the extent to which the scores measure the underlying construct (i.e., validity). Reliability is indexed by three methods: test–retest, parallel forms, and internal consistency (McDonald, 1999). Test–retest reliability reflects the extent to which the same individual obtains the same score when given the same test. Alternate forms reliability reflects the extent to which the same individual obtains the same scores when given a test with different but equivalent items. Internal consistency indicates the extent to which the indicators are consistent with the total score within a scale. It is used as a measure of reliability under the assumption that high internal consistency can only occur when people with similar attributes respond the same way across the items and the items are good indicators of that summary score.

Validity reflects the extent to which summary scores measure the underlying construct (McDonald, 1999). To establish validity, the researcher must find an alternative measure of that construct and demonstrate that the summary measure is highly related to the alternative measure. Scores from the measure are correlated with scores from other instruments believed to measure the same construct (concurrent and convergent validity), other instruments believed to measure similar but distinct constructs (discriminant validity), and criterion variables theorized to be associated with the construct of interest (criterion and predictive validity). The goal is to establish a credible case that the measure is indeed measuring the intended construct and only the intended construct. Group difference studies can be particularly helpful in this regard when members of groups with known characteristics (ideally characteristics measured with little or no measurement error) can be distinguished in predicable ways given knowledge of their test scores. In addition, there are two nonstatistical types of validity. Face validity is the extent to which individuals feel that the items are reflect the underlying construct. Content validity is the extent to which there was a clear articulated plan used to develop the indicators based on the quantification of the underlying construct.

CTT has been used to develop a generation of educational and psychological instruments (McDonald, 1999). This approach provided clear rules and a good foundation for measurement. However, it was clear there were many issues this approach did not handle well. First, there was an unfortunate tendency to believe that reliability and validity were inherent properties of the instruments. Logically, it is obvious that an instrument can only be used reliably and validly when prior work demonstrated those properties for the population being sampled for a given study (Standard 15.1, AERA et al., 1999). This problem was not inherent to the approach, but with the failure to assure reliability and validity for each population assessed with an instrument. Perhaps more problematic was the reliance on factor analysis for development and correlations for demonstrating the reliability and validity of measures with ordinal or nominal items. Almost all educational and psychological tests rely on nominal items (pass/fail) and almost all questionnaires rely on ordinal Likert-type questions, but they do not provide good measures of covariance, which is at the heart of factor analysis. In addition, CTT often assumes that the precision of the test, like the reliability, is uniform across all levels of the construct. This is almost certainly untrue because these tests yield much less information about individuals at either end of the distribution. Finally, the need for shorter, more efficient measures drove educators in particular to seek methods that can reliably measure constructs with fewer, not more, indicators. Newer methods, such as IRT, provide statistical methods for developing tests that address these issues.

IRT

IRT was developed to address some of the problems encountered with CTT by generating assessment models that accommodate nominal or ordinal items (Embretson, 1996). As such, the method offers greater precision of measurement with shorter assessment tools. IRT is now widely used for educational testing and is becoming more commonly used to develop psychological assessments for research and clinical settings (Embretson, 1996; Embretson & Reise, 2000; Thissen, 1993). Educational tests developed with IRT include the Scholastic Assessment Test, the Graduate Record Examinations, and the test that states use to address the No Child Left Behind mandates.

The goal of the remainder of this chapter is to provide a brief and nontechnical introduction to the concepts behind IRT and present several benefits of using IRT techniques. These benefits include performing detailed item analysis, assessing item bias, assessing scale dimensionality, linking scales, and administering adaptive tests. This treatment is by no means exhaustive; instead we intend to outline for the reader the reasons it is to their advantage to add IRT techniques to their measurement toolbox. Embretson and Reise (2000) offer a more complete introduction to IRT and a comparison between CTT and IRT (see also Lord & Novick, 1968; McDonald, 1999; Thissen, 1993). For further details, there are several excellent sources that provide thorough explanations of the mathematical and technical details behind IRT (Baker, 1985; Bock, 1997; McDonald, 1999; Thissen & Wainer, 2001).

Brief Description of IRT

IRT is a collection of statistical models and techniques used to fit categorical responses to items. The most frequently chosen IRT model is similar to the logistic regression model, with one major exception: the predictor is a single latent variable, which represents the underlying construct. This latent variable is referred to as the "theta" or "ability" or "person" parameter in the IRT literature (Embretson & Reise, 2000).

Commonly available IRT software was designed to fit a unidimensional, or single, latent variable; however, recent developments allow for the fitting of multivariate latent traits, appropriately called multidimensional IRT (Reckase, 1997). For example, M-Plus (Muthén & Muthén, 2005) now allows for estimating item parameters and latent ability scores for multiple dimensions, and assessing the fit to determine whether more or fewer dimensions are needed. These methods can be used when you are concerned that a scale is not unidimensional or to ascertain the dimensionality of the instrument (see Bock, Gibbons, & Muraki, 1988; Muthén, 1978).

As in logistic regression, the outcome, or dependent variable, is the logit transformation of the odds. For a binary item, the odds are simply the probability of responding yes divided by the probability of responding no. Essentially the probability of responding yes to an item is modeled as an exponential function of the single latent ability. This procedure can be viewed as analogous to a one-factor analysis model for binary indicators (McDonald, 1999). In IRT, the latent ability must also be estimated, and, as in traditional factor analysis, the distribution of the latent ability is assumed to be standard normal.

The number of parameters used to describe the shape of the functional relationship between the probability of responding yes to a binary item and the latent variable distinguishes the types of models presented in the IRT literature (McDonald, 1999). These parameters are referred to as item parameters and, unless constrained to be equal, are specific to an individual item. The Rasch model, or one-parameter logistic (1-PL) IRT model, allows for one additional parameter over the latent ability parameter and is analogous to an intercept in a multiple regression model. The point on the latent ability scale where the odds are 50:50 that a person responds yes is defined as the intercept. This point is also known as the difficulty, location, threshold, or "b" parameter. Because the latent ability scale is centered at the mode (i.e., standard normal), when the estimated difficulty parameter is at "0," the odds are 50:50 that a person having an average level of the latent ability will respond yes. If the difficulty parameter is −1, then a person one unit below average on the latent ability has a 50:50 chance of responding yes, while a person of average ability will have greater odds. Hence, this parameter locates the item on the latent variable scale.

An additional parameter is used in the two-parameter (2-PL) IRT model. This parameter represents an estimate of the strength of the linear relationship between the logit and the latent ability and is analogous to the loading in a one-factor analytic model for binary items (McDonald, 1999; Muthén, 1978). Therefore, in IRT, the actual relationship between the probability of responding yes and the latent trait is modeled as nonlinear. This second item parameter is also known by several names in the IRT literature: discrimination, slope, or "a" parameter. A third parameter can be used to represent the lower asymptote in the functional relationship and is referred to as "c" or the guessing parameter.

Simultaneously estimating item parameters and a single latent trait parameter requires sophisticated and complex techniques, along with a great deal of computational power. These estimation methods are beyond the scope of this paper, but an interested reader can find details in Baker (1985).

Benefits of IRT

Item Analysis and Scale Development

The IRT model-based approach has proven to be extremely useful in item analysis and scale development. IRT methods allow for shortening tests without sacrificing precision, can convey information about specific behaviors, and can be used with individuals with missing data. Each of these characteristics is a consequence of linking items directly to the estimated latent ability score instead of indirectly though the total raw score in CTT (Embretson & Reise, 2000). Once the item parameters are estimated, then a subset of the items can be used to target specific levels of the latent trait. More importantly, the precision of measurement under IRT is specified uniquely for each level of the latent trait as a direct consequence of the statistical modeling techniques (called "information"). Scales can be built to target certain levels of a trait precisely by identifying the items that best measure that trait at that level. Finally, because items are linked to ability scores, you can estimate ability even when some items are missing.

Assessing Item and Scale Bias

Accuracy and fairness are critical dimensions in the development of instruments that are used clinically to make decisions that impact children's lives. IRT methods allow for a direct assessment of whether an item or scale is biased across different populations and, therefore, are especially useful in examining the cultural sensitivity of the instrument. Bias occurs when individuals with comparable skill levels on the underlying construct receive different ability scores because the items work differently in different populations. Hence, the different subgroups have different probabilities of making a correct response (Holland & Wainer, 1993). This investigation has become known as differential item functioning (DIF) and differential test functioning (DTF) (Raju, 1988; Raju, van der Linden, & Fleer, 1995). DIF methods use model estimates of the difference between item and test characteristic curves while matching the underlying ability level of the respondents. An item or test is considered biased if individuals with the same ability level have different probabilities of responding in a particular direction.

Assessing Person Fit

Another advantage IRT offers is the possibility of assessing person fit, that is, the degree to which the instrument is useful in measuring an individual (Embretson & Reise, 2000). Several indices have been proposed in the literature (for a detailed review of the current person-fit indices, see Meijer, 1996). Essentially, each index offers a method for determining whether an individual's response pattern is statistically consistent with a valid response pattern of a person having that ability level. This can be useful in determining aberrant response patterns.

Linking Scales Across Versions

Because IRT can handle missing response patterns on a collection of items, the linking of scales is more easily implemented than in CTT approaches (Holland & Rubin, 1982). As long as a subset of examinees respond to a subset of overlapping items, then the item parameters can be computed and the latent trait can be estimated for an individual with that skill level through a process called equating (Lee, 2003). IRT offers model-based methods that include item difficulty and person ability estimates in the analysis and thus provide a more informative look at the relationship between different measures of the same construct and different forms of the same measure. For example, if one wanted to scale several versions of a test on a single latent trait, then each version can contain different items as long as a subset of items remain identical. There is no technically equivalent method in the classical tradition beyond the use of expert opinion and descriptive statistics—practices that do not guarantee that the different tests will yield comparable scores for individuals with comparable skills (Bond & Fox, 2001). This property is especially important with clinical instruments such as annual academic assessments used to determine whether children have learned enough to be promoted because their validity depends on exact equating of tests across different versions.

Adaptive Testing

Finally, IRT offers a clear advantage to traditional psychometric methods in the adaptive testing arena, particularly if administered by a computerized platform (computer adaptive testing, CAT; see Wainer, 1990). Once items are identified by their item parameters as accurate measures on a specific level of a latent trait, pools of items can be combined to target the entire range of the trait. Selected items from the pool can be administered in a fashion that more efficiently targets an individual. IRT applications to existing tests that require interviewers to use basal and ceiling items may make the administration of these tests more efficient and accurate (Daniel, 1999). As computers become more widely used for data collection, scales that are specifically developed for CAT administration should be included. At this point, only large testing companies have undertaken the task of collecting item pools and administering CATs (Embretson & Reise, 2000), but future research is likely to lessen the burden put on a teacher or parent by using a CAT-developed test to more efficiently target the behavior or aptitude of a child rather than administering over 50 items that were clearly off-target.

EXAMPLE

Data from the Preschool Learning Behaviors Scale (PLBS) (McDermott et al., 2000) were scored using both CTT and IRT to demonstrate the two approaches. The scale was designed to measure the approaches to learning construct in young children based on teacher report. The PLBS is based on extensive research and development using the methods of classical measurement theory. McDermott (2002) found distinct and reliable scale scores for the PLBS based on sample results of factor analyses. Further, the authors reported correlations that provided validity evidence based on convergence with indices of social skills and divergence from measures of problem behaviors. Its use across a number of studies has established evidence of technical merit in national studies of Head Start children (e.g., Zill, 2006). Data from the example are from the fall assessment in an intervention study designed to improve approaches to learning among 477 low-income preschoolers within an urban Head Start program (Lambert, Abbott-Shim, Vanderweile, & O'Donell, 2006).

CTT scores were computed based on the instrument scoring guidelines. The sum of the items for the four scale scores was computed and transformed into t-scores (i.e., norming sample mean of 50 and $SD = 10$) through using the tables provided by the instrument developer. The items and summary scores showed considerable negative skewness, similar to the norming sample. Reliability was estimated using internal consistency and ranged from .58 to .83. The first column of Table 1 describes these scores.

IRT scores were computed using a one-parameter logistic model (i.e., a Rasch model). These scores were computed using IRT software and using a hierarchical linear modeling (HLM) approach (Raudenbush & Bryk, 2001). Using an IRT software program, WINSTEPS (Linacre & Wright, 2000), we fitted a Rasch model and obtained an estimate of ability for each child and of difficulty for each item. The reliability was indexed by the capacity of the IRT model to index ability for each individual. The reliabilities (.36–.67) were worse for the Rasch scores than for the CTT, reflecting the fact that many children displayed none of the behavior indicated by the items. Concerned about the instrument's ability to measure children at the lower end of the distribution, the item parameters (i.e., difficulty) were examined for the first scale, Competence Motivation. The estimated item difficulties indicated that none of the items was especially useful in measuring children with higher or lower ability levels. Because of this, the reliability in estimating ability scores for children at either level is low, and, therefore, the average reliability across the skill distribution is lower than in CTT, which does not take this problem into account.

The HLM approach provides a useful method for estimating scores that are comparable to those produced by the one-parameter logistic IRT model because it accommodates the dependencies in the data associated with having teachers rate multiple children within the classroom. This approach involved creating a three-level HLM to allow for clustering of items within a given child and clustering of children within the classroom. HLM explicitly acknowledges the implicit dependencies related to having teachers rate children on multiple items, and actually accounting for the possible

TABLE 1

ESTIMATED SCORES AND RELIABILITIES FROM CLASSICAL TEST THEORY (CTT), ITEM RESPONSE THEORY (IRT), AND HIERARCHICAL LINEAR MODELING (HLM) SCORING OF PRESCHOOL BEHAVIOR LEARNING SCALE

| | | Raw Scores | CTT | | IRT (Rasch) | | HLM (Analogous to 1-PL IRT) | | |
	# Items	Mean	Mean (SD)	Reliability	Mean (SD)	Reliability	Mean	Reliability Child Level	Reliability Class Level
Competence motivation	11	16.6	48.4 (10.2)	.83	69.0 (16.2)	.67	16.9	.75	.81
Persistence-attention	8	12.8	48.3 (11.1)	.82	68.8 (16.3)	.71	13.0	.76	.77
Attitude toward learning	5	10.7	49.3 (13.3)	.67	67.9 (16.3)	.49	10.8	.55	.80
Strategy-flexibility	4	6.0	48.0 (10.4)	.58	71.7 (16.3)	.36	6.1	.32	.86

Note.—Mean scores are computed using different metrics. The CTT scores are norm-referenced *t* scores. The IRT scores are within-sample "ability" estimates. The HLM scores are estimated raw scores.

37

informant effect if teachers use the rating scale differently. The model estimates an ability latent variability for each child using the items as indicators. The loadings of each item are fixed to be 1, making this analogous to a one-parameter IRT model. Although estimates of ability scores were similar across the two model specifications, the HLM analysis also indicated that differences in how teachers use the rating scale could be masking true differences among children. The lower reliability at the child level than at the class level indicates there is good precision to compare classroom means, even if we do not have good precision in measuring the individual child.

A comparison of the results from scoring this scale using CTT and IRT suggests that the PLBS may not be appropriate for all 4-year-olds and that there might be a teacher effect influencing scores as computed using either CTT or IRT. The correlations among the estimated scaled scores across the methods were quite high ($r > .90$). The reliabilities were highest with CTT, but CTT ignored the fact that much less information was available to score children's learning approaches when teachers rated them at the bottom of the scale—which, unfortunately, happened frequently. In fact, examination of the item characteristics using IRT indicated that the CTT reliability is probably inflated when the instrument is used with children with low or high levels of learning approaches.

CONCLUSIONS AND IMPLICATIONS FOR DEVELOPMENTAL RESEARCH

Development of a new instrument entails careful examination of the construct to be measured, a clear definition of the population to be assessed, and the careful development of indicators or items. Both CTT and IRT provide clear guidelines for developing instruments, starting with selecting indicators and ending with scoring. Instrument development is difficult work and requires careful attention and a great of time. Developmentalists should not embark on generating their own instruments unless they have sufficient psychometric expertise and resources in terms of both time and money.

Contrasts between CTT and IRT suggest that they are not completely different, but that IRT offers several advantages. As in our example, summary scores from IRT and CTT analyses of measures created using a CTT framework are often highly correlated because the instruments were usually developed with approximately equally discriminating items (i.e., items designed to provide good assessment at the middle level of the ability distribution). Therefore, it is unlikely that applying IRT to existing scales will yield great increases in precision because the greatest increase in precision with IRT relates to using items of varying difficulty. In contrast, scales developed through IRT promise greater precision across all skill levels in tests that consist of fewer items, and can be equated across versions. These characteristics are especially important when instruments are used for clinical purposes, and the scores have implications for the lives of children.

ACKNOWLEDGMENTS

Partial funding for this effort was provided by the Agency for Children, Youth, and Families, U.S. Department of Health and Human Services, through a grant entitled Head Start Quality Research Center.

REFERENCES

American Educational Research Association, American Psychological Association, & National Council on Measurement in Education. (1999). *Standards for educational and psychological testing*. Washington, DC: Author.

Baker, F. (1985). *Item response theory: Parameter estimation techniques*. New York: Marcel Dekker.

Bock, R. D. (1997). A brief history of item response theory. *Educational Measurement: Issues and Practice*, **16**, 21–33.

Bock, R. D., Gibbons, R., & Muraki, E. J. (1988). Full information item factor analysis. *Applied Psychological Measurement*, **12**, 261–280.

Bond, T. G., & Fox, C. M. (2001). *Applying the rasch model: Fundamental measurement in the human sciences*. Mahwah, NJ: Lawrence Erlbaum Associates.

Bredekamp, S., & Copple, C. (Eds.). (1997). *Developmentally appropriate practice in early childhood programs* (rev. ed.). Washington, DC: National Association for the Education of Young Children.

Daniel, M. H. (1999). Behind the Scenes: Using new measurement methods on DAS and KAIT. In S. Embretson & S. L. Hershberger (Eds.), *The new rules of measurement: What every psychologists and educator should know* (pp. 37–64). Mahwah, NJ: Lawrence Erlbaum Associates Inc.

Embretson, S. E. (1996). The new rules of measurement. *Psychological Assessment*, **8** (4), 341–349.

Embretson, S. E., & Reise, S. (2000). *Item response theory for psychologists*. Mahwah, NJ: Lawrence Erlbaum Associates.

Greenspan, S. I., Meisels, S., Barnard, K., Barrera, I., Berman, C., & Bricker, D., et al. (1994). Toward a new vision for the developmental assessment of infants and young children. *Zero to Three*, **14** (6), 22.

Holland, P. W., & Rubin, D. (1982). *Test equating*. New York: Academic Press.

Holland, P. W., & Wainer, H. (1993). *Differential item functioning*. Hillsdale, NJ: Lawrence Erlbaum Associates.

Lambert, R., Abbott-Shim, M., & Sibley, A. (2006). Evaluating the quality of early childhood educational settings. In B. Spodek & O. N. Saracho (Eds.), *Handbook of research on the education of young children* (2nd ed., pp. 457–470). Mahwah, NJ: Lawrence Erlbaum Associates.

Lambert, R., Abbott-Shim, M., VandeWiele, L., & O'Donnell, M. (2006). *An evaluation of the individualized learning intervention: Mentoring program for early childhood teachers*. Paper to be presented at the meeting of the American Educational Research Association, San Diego, CA.

Lee, O. K. (2003). Rasch simultaneous vertical equating for measuring reading growth. *Journal of Applied Measurement*, **4**, 10–23.

Linacre, J. M., & Wright, B. D. (2000). *WINSTEPS: Multiple choice, rating scale, and partial credit Rasch analysis [Computer software]*. Chicago: MESA.

Lord, F. M. (1977). Practical applications of item characteristic curve theory. *Journal of Educational Measurement*, **14**, 117–138.

Lord, F. M., & Novick, M. R. (1968). *Statistical theories of mental test scores*. Reading, MA: Addison-Wesley.

McDermott, P. (2002). Preschool learning behaviors scale: Development and validation of the preschool learning behaviors scale. *Psychology in the Schools*, **39** (4), 353–365.

McDermott, P. A., Green, L. F., Francis, J. M., & Stott, D. H. (2000). *Preschool learning behaviors scale*. Philadelphia: Edumetric and Clinical Science.

McDonald, R. P. (1999). *Test theory: A unified treatment*. Mahwah, NJ: Lawrence Erlbaum Associates.

McLean, M., Wolery, M., & Bailey, D. (2004). *Assessing infants and preschoolers with special needs*. Upper Saddle River, NJ: Merrill Prentice Hall.

Meijer, R. R. (1996). Person-fit research: An introduction. *Applied Measurement in Education*, **9**, 3–8.

Muthén, B. (1978). Contributions to factor analysis of dichotomous items. *Psychometrika*, **43**, 551–560.

Muthén, B., & Muthén, L. (2005). *Mplus Users Manual Version 3.12*. Los Angeles, CA: Muthén & Muthén.

National Association for the Education of Young Children. (2003). *Position Statement: Early childhood curriculum, assessment, and program evaluation*. Retrieved January 15, 2005, from http://www.naeyc.org/about/positions.asp

Nunnally, J. C., & Bernstein, I. H. (1994). *Psychometric theory* (3rd ed.). New York: McGraw-Hill.

Pretti-Frontczak, K., Kowalksi, K., & Brown, R. D. (2002). Preschool teachers' use of assessment and curricula: A statewide examination. *Exceptional Children*, **69**, 109–123.

Raju, N. S. (1988). The area between two item characteristic curves. *Psychometrika*, **53**, 495–502.

Raju, N., van der Linden, W. J., & Fleer, P. (1995). IRT-based internal measures of differential functioning of items and tests. *Applied Psychological Measurement*, **19** (4), 353–368.

Raudenbush, S. W., & Bryk, A. S. (2001). *Hierarchical linear models: Applications and data analysis methods* (2nd ed.). Newbury Park, CA: Sage Publications.

Reckase, M. D. (1997). The past and future of multidimensional item response theory. *Applied Psychological Measurement*, **21**, 25–36.

Stevens, S. S. (1948). On the theory of scales of measurement. *Science*, **103**, 677–680.

Thissen, D. (1993). Repealing rules that no longer apply to psychological measurement. In N. Frederiksen, R. J. Mislevy & I. I. Bejar (Eds.), *Test theory for a new generation of tests* (pp. 79–97). Hillsdale, NJ: Lawerence Erlbaum Associates.

Thissen, D., & Wainer, H. (2001). *Test scoring*. Mahwah, NJ: Lawrence Erlbaum Associates.

Wainer, H. (1990). *Computerized adaptive testing: A primer.* Hillsdale, NJ: Lawrence Erlbaum Associates.

Wilson, M. (2005). *Constructing measures: An item response modeling approach.* Mahwah, NJ: Lawerence Erlbaum Associates.

Zill, N. (2006, January). *Expanding the scope of the National Reporting System to cover information on social-emotional development and child health.* Paper presented at the quarterly meeting of the Head Start Quality Research Consortium, Washington, DC.

III. MISSING DATA: WHAT TO DO WITH OR WITHOUT THEM

Most statistical techniques presented in standard courses on statistical methods in undergraduate and graduate social science programs presume the presence of complete data. In class after class, research scenarios are presented that can be analyzed using t-tests of mean differences from independent or dependent samples, z-tests or t-tests of correlations, analysis of variance using one-way or multi-way designs, or other techniques. Because these scenarios are usually idealized examples, the issue of missing data is rarely, if ever, confronted. However, in conducting developmental research, particularly longitudinal investigations, the presence of missing data is the rule, not the exception. Practicing scientists design research studies fully committed to obtaining complete responses by each participant to all questions at each time of measurement, knowing that the likelihood of accomplishing this goal is essentially zero. Because missing data are expected in longitudinal studies, questions naturally arise regarding how to analyze data to arrive at the least biased representation of developmental trends.

Research on modern approaches to dealing with missing data began three decades ago, spurred by a framework developed by Rubin (1976). Then, about two decades ago, several important papers and books were published, including Little and Rubin (1987) and Rubin (1987). The preceding books provided what were then state-of-the-art techniques to deal with missing data, but more importantly set out issues to be investigated further. During the past 20 years, a great deal of quantitative work has focused on the myriad issues occasioned by missing data.

The present chapter is introductory in nature, designed to acquaint researchers with broad issues related to treatment of missing data. The literature on missing data techniques is very extensive and confronts many complex issues, so the practicing scientist must consult other sources to understand how to apply missing data procedures in their research, as a tutorial on how to apply missing data techniques is beyond the scope of the current chapter. My aims are to (a) discuss origins of missing data, (b) define three types of missing data, (c) describe common data analysis options for longitudinal investigations that have missing data, (d) identify three general approaches to handling missing data, (e) describe eight alternative strategies for dealing with missing data, together with a brief rendition of the relative strengths and weaknesses of each approach, (f) demonstrate the different patterns in results that arise using various ways of handling missing data to reinforce the importance of the choice of a proper method, and (g) provide recommendations about how researchers should deal with missing values in their own research. In addition, key references are provided to good introductions or summaries of issues related to missing data.

ORIGINS AND TYPES OF MISSING DATA

Origins of Missing Data

Missing values on items for particular respondents can arise in many ways, and outlining these ways can help in both defining the nature and extent of the problem and choosing ways of dealing with the missing values. In this section, I discuss four of these origins of missing data under the headings of item nonresponse, scale nonresponse, time of measurement nonresponse, and failure to assess participants at intermediate times.

Item Nonresponse

In any research study, a participant may fail to have a registered response to a particular item. This item nonresponse can be due to any of several processes. For example, the participant may have a minor, transitory lapse in attention, leading to skipping a given item, which is especially likely if items are presented at a predetermined rate. Or the participant may decide not to answer a particular item, wanting to think more about how to register a response, and then forget to return later to the item and complete a response. Or the item may inquire about information that the participant feels is quite personal, so the participant might decide not to respond to such an "extreme" item. Of course, a missing response to a single item might result from a mechanical error, such as the poor "bubbling in" of an answer option on a machine-readable answer sheet, leading the optical scanner to fail to identify a response for the item. Any of these processes—or others not discussed—can be the basis for an item nonresponse for an individual participant, and missing item responses lead to difficulties in placing the participant on the dimension assessed by the set of items. But, if the respondent has item responses on other items from the scale, a researcher could use these responses to help supply a reasonable estimate of missing responses for certain items, as discussed below.

Scale Nonresponse

In addition to item nonresponse, a participant may fail to complete all items in a particular questionnaire or instrument. Sometimes scale nonresponse arises from accidental failure to assemble a full instrument protocol; at other times, scale nonresponse occurs because data are collected across several closely spaced visits and the participant misses one or more visits. Or a participant may simply not have sufficient time to complete all instruments or assessment devices in a research protocol, so scales placed later in the protocol are not completed. Regardless of the reason, no responses on any of the scale items are available for the particular respondent. With scale nonresponse, any attempt to derive a meaningful estimate of the participant's position on the dimension assessed by the scale would be based on information from other scales obtained at the same time or a different time of measurement.

Time of Measurement Nonresponse, or Drop-Out

One of the most common reasons for missing data in a longitudinal study can be termed time of measurement nonresponse, or drop-out. Virtually all longitudinal studies suffer from the drop-out of some participants. Various methods have been developed to reduce the incidence of drop-out, such as the use of birthday cards or newsletters that convey new results from the study to increase participant interest in the study. Work on patterns of attrition in longitudinal studies (e.g., Levin, Katzen, Klein, & Llabre, 2000; Siddiqui, Flay, & Hu, 1996) typically finds that persons who drop-out of a longitudinal study tend to have lower levels of positive characteristics and higher levels of negative characteristics. For example, Siddiqui et al. (1996), in a longitudinal study of smoking prevention, found that drop-outs tended to have lower levels of academic achievement and higher levels of cigarette smoking and marijuana use. Knowing about factors that differentially affect participant attrition can help guide efforts to retain participants likely to drop out. Still, the presence of nontrivial levels of attrition is the norm in longitudinal studies.

Failure to Assess at Crucial or Intermediate Points

To reinforce the importance of missing data, one should consider the fact that data are collected in most longitudinal studies on a fixed schedule, such as annually. Because of this, all data on all participants on all variables are completely missing at all intermediate points in time. Seen from this vantage point, only a fraction of all possible data are collected in any longitudinal study, even if attrition were miniscule or absent. This observation might be dismissed as a trivial truism, but I included it here to reinforce at least two matters. First, the times of measurement in any longitudinal study should be chosen based on hypotheses regarding development of the processes under study and ideas about the optimal causal lag among variables (cf. Burchinal & Appelbaum, 1991; Collins, 2006; Gollob & Reichardt, 1987; McArdle & Epstein, 1987), rather than on either historical standards in the field or the vagaries of funding opportunities. Second, and more importantly here, any method of handling missing data relies on assumptions regarding the mechanisms underlying missingness and assumptions regarding patterns in results we would have observed had we had access to the missing values. If the assumptions associated with a particular method of handling missing data are difficult to justify, then another, more acceptable method should be sought.

Types of Missing Data

In addition to the origins of missing data, a second way to describe missing values is with regard to the statistical relations associated with the missingness. In work on missing data, three categories of missingness are usually distinguished: missing completely at random (MCAR), missing at random, and nonignorable missingness.

MCAR

Data can be characterized as MCAR if the missingness, or the probability of missing data, on an outcome variable Y_j ($j = 1, \ldots, j, \ldots, p$) is unrelated (a) to the value of Y_j itself or (b) to values on any of the remaining ($p-1$) variables in the data. To study this issue, one could create a dummy variable with a value of 0 if an individual had a missing value on Y_j or a 1 if the individual had a valid, nonmissing value on Y_j. If this index variable were statistically unrelated to all remaining variables in the data set, then condition (b) above would be satisfied, although small sample size may lead to low power to detect such relations. Unfortunately, condition (a) cannot be tested because we do not have access to the values on Y_j for persons with missing values on this variable.

Missing at Random

Data are missing at random (MAR) if the probability of missing data on Y_j is unrelated to the value of Y_j after controlling statistically for other variables in the analysis. One way to deal with this problem is to identify whether the probability of missingness on a given outcome variable Y_j is related to any of the remaining variables in the data set. If missingness on Y_j is related to other variables, then these other variables must be included in any analysis of variable Y_j to correct for biases in parameter estimates that would otherwise occur.

Nonignorable Missingness

The third type of missingness is termed nonignorable missingness. Missingness is identified as nonignorable if the missing values on Y_j are related to Y_j even after controlling statistically other variables in the data set. Nonignorable missingness will most often occur in extant data sets that inadvertently fail to include variables that other studies have found to be related to missingness on Y_j. Methods of analysis for nonignorable missing data are beyond the scope of the present chapter, but Little and Rubin (2002) and Allison (2002) contain discussions of such methods.

ANALYTIC OPTIONS FOR HANDLING MISSING DATA

Classical Longitudinal Data Analysis Methods

Methods for the analysis of longitudinal data have evolved to a stunning extent during the past 30 years or more. Before that time, choices among alternative statistical techniques were limited, and the options available in statistical computer programs were also quite limited. Today, a wealth of statistical models can be used, and computer programs are increasingly adaptable in the fitting of models. However, practicing researchers in most areas of psychology, including developmental psychology, often rely on older, tried and true methods. Among these tried and true methods are typical ways of handling missing data, which are usually adopted implicitly through defaults in computer programs and which, unbeknownst to the researcher, may lead to less-than-optimal representations of data.

To illustrate what may be called classical longitudinal data analysis methods, I will refer in this section to the Nesselroade and Baltes (1974) study, a standard-setting cross-sequential study. In this study, Nesselroade and Baltes provided clear justifications for their analyses that were designed, in part, to assess the impact of missing data on results from the study.

Longitudinal Comparisons

The principal aim of most longitudinal comparisons is to study mean levels of age-related changes in behavior as well as individual differences in age-related changes. Hence, longitudinal comparisons are the principal, core analyses in most longitudinal studies. In their major analyses, Nesselroade and Baltes (1974) eliminated all participants who had dropped out of the study after the first time of measurement and analyzed only data from persons who participated at all three points of measurement. In these analyses, Nesselroade and Baltes concentrated on analyzing and interpreting patterns of mean change across time on each of several outcome variables.

Drop-Out Control Comparisons

Drop-out control comparisons seek to determine differences on study variables between those who stayed in the longitudinal study across all times of measurement and participants who dropped out at some point after the first time of measurement. Nesselroade and Baltes (1974) calculated drop-out control comparisons by computing t-tests of mean difference for stayers versus drop-outs on all variables collected at Time 1, and they then attempted to restrict generalization of longitudinal results if differences arose in the drop-out control analyses.

Retest Control Comparisons

Retest control comparisons are designed to estimate the effect of re-testing on participants' scores. Often, it appears that retesting participants two or more times on a given instrument can lead to alterations in their scores, such as otherwise unaccountable rises in intelligence test scores over a short test–retest interval. Nesselroade and Baltes (1974) compared performance at Time 3 for the "stayers" against performance by retest control participants, who were persons from the same cohorts tested at the same point in time but tested for the first time on all measures. If retesting effects were not present, then stayers and retest control participants should perform similarly on all measures.

Assumptions

The principal assumption of longitudinal comparisons based on only those participants with complete data is that the resulting analyses of stayers capture or estimate the population parameters that generated the data. This assumption is directly challenged by studies of drop-outs, such as those cited above (Levin et al., 2000; Siddiqui et al., 1996), which typically find that persons who drop-out of longitudinal studies differ systematically from those who remain in the study across all waves of measurement. If drop-outs differ from those who stay in for the full study, then parameters based on only those who participate at all waves will generally be positively biased to an unknown extent.

Owing to questions regarding the preceding assumption, a second key assumption is invoked in connection with the drop-out control comparisons and retest control comparisons. This assumption holds that that we, as researchers or as consumers of research, can limit generalizations properly if significant differences on either set of comparisons are found. Whether this assumption is met in practice is open for debate. Clearly, researchers often add caveats in discussing implications of their research, but whether this is sufficient to enable readers to interpret results correctly often cannot be determined.

Using hindsight, better ways of analyzing data are now available that either circumvent the potentially problematic assumptions associated with the Nesselroade and Baltes (1974) analyses or can evaluate those assumptions. Rather than performing a series of analyses (e.g., longitudinal comparisons, drop-out comparisons, etc.), newer methods of analysis would include all participants in a single series of analyses, potentially using multiple-group modeling strategies. Thus, McArdle and Hamagami (1991) described how to define different groups based on their patterns of missingness to derive less-biased estimates of parameters. In addition, work by McArdle and his colleagues (e.g., McArdle & Woodcock, 1997; Ferrer, Salthouse, Stewart, & Schwartz, 2004; Ferrer, Salthouse, McArdle, Stewart, & Schwartz, 2005) has demonstrated interesting ways to incorporate the modeling of retest effects into longitudinal investigations. These newer methods accept the fact that missing data will occur and use the presence of missing data to ask questions that illuminate general developmental processes as well as processes associated with attrition and retesting.

General Approaches to Handling Missing Data

In the presence of missing data, at least three general approaches to dealing with the missing data can be identified. Consider a typical data matrix in which the rows of the matrix represent observations (or persons) and the columns of the matrix denote variables; a complete data set would have a nonmissing value on each variable for each observation. The first of the three general approaches to handing missing data is covered by the term deletion. Under a deletion strategy, the researcher deletes rows (i.e., observations, or persons) or columns (i.e., items or scales) that contain missing data. Once the rows and/or columns that contain missing values are deleted, one is left with a matrix of reduced size, but one with a nonmissing value for each observation in each column.

A second approach can be identified as *substitution*. Substitution refers to replacing each missing value with a particular, specifiable value based on nonmissing values in the same column or row of the data matrix or on information gleaned from other columns of the matrix. The key to identifying a method as employing substitution is whether the same identical value would be used as substitute for missing data if one repeated the process.

The third general approach can be termed *imputation*, in which a representative value is inserted for each missing value, a representative value that preserves the multivariate structure of relations among variables in the data set. Imputation can be either explicit or implicit. Explicit imputation occurs when a given, representative value is included in a data set in place of a missing value. In contrast, what I have called implicit imputation occurs when a model is fit to raw data in a fashion that uses all available nonmissing values and assumes that missing values would conform to patterns of results obtained with the nonmissing values.

Eight Alternative Strategies

In this section, eight alternative strategies for dealing with missing data will be discussed, strategies that variously implement the general deletion, substitution, or imputation approaches discussed above. The first five methods described below comprise deletion and substitution strategies; they are relatively common approaches that, at times, can be beneficial but are not generally recommended as methods for dealing with missing data. The final three methods are variants of imputation strategies; these more modern methods for coping with missing values represent state-of-the-art techniques that should find more use in current research situations.

Listwise Deletion

Listwise deletion consists of the deletion of each observation (e.g., person) that has missing data on any of the variables in the data set or in a particular analysis. Listwise deletion is a common default in most computer programs for many standard forms of analysis. For example, with multiple regression analysis, most computer programs delete all observations with missing values on the criterion variable or on any of the predictor variables when estimating that individual regression analysis.

One benefit of listwise deletion is that a common base—the set of observations with complete data—is used for estimating all basic statistics, including means, *SD*s, and correlations. However, if this restricted group is explicitly or implicitly selected in some fashion (i.e., tend to score higher on positively oriented variables), then all statistics will be biased estimates of population parameters. Furthermore, as sample size is decreased by deleting observations with missing values, power to detect differences and precision of estimates will be reduced. Finally, if many analyses are performed, different analyses will often be conducted on different sample sizes based on the subset of variables included in the particular analysis, making comparisons of results across analyses difficult. Thus, key assumptions involve the representativeness of the reduced sample with complete data and the unimportance of the decrease in power and precision due to reduced sample size.

Pairwise Deletion

Pairwise deletion refers to the deletion of all observations that have missing values on either of a pair of variables analyzed. For example, if one calculated correlations among variables X_1–X_{10}, each of the resulting 45 unique correlations might be based on a different sample size, as the correlation between any two variables is calculated on all observations with nonmissing values on the pair of variables. This is the standard option in most popular computer programs when computing all correlations among a set of variables.

The most obvious strength of pairwise deletion is that all possible information represented in the nonmissing values is used when calculating particular statistics, such as means, *SD*s, and correlations. However, because each statistic estimated using pairwise deletion may be based on a different sample size, providing a valid numerical summary that accurately reflects the entire sample is probably impossible. Furthermore, correlation matrices computed using pairwise deletion frequently do not have inverses, precluding their use for many common forms of analysis including regression analysis and confirmatory factor analysis.

Sample Mean Substitution

Sample mean substitution is a procedure by which all missing values on a given measure, whether an item or a scale score, are replaced by the sample mean for that measure. This is a common default in computer programs for replacement of missing values.

One strength of mean substitution is the fact that this method leaves the sample mean of nonmissing values unchanged. Moreover, the mean is often touted as the value in a univariate distribution that best describes the location, or midpoint, of the distribution. However, mean substitution must lead to a negative bias of the *SD* of a variable, as every observation having the mean inserted in place of a missing value will fall precisely at the mean and therefore have a null-squared deviation from the mean. Further, mean substitution must decrease the correlation of a variable with all other variables in the data set. The Pearson product moment correlation is computed using the product of the deviation of the *X* and *Y* scores from their respective means. Because mean substitution replaces a missing value with the mean for the variable, any observation with a mean substituted for missing data must have a null deviation from the mean, reducing the value in the numerator of any correlation involving the variable. Given these shortcomings, sample mean substitution should, in general, not be used as a method of replacing missing data.

Individual Mean Substitution

Individual mean substitution is another common method of replacing missing values. If an observation has nonmissing values for many or most items on a scale (e.g., nonmissing values for eight of 10 items), then calculating the mean of nonmissing values is essentially identical to substitution of the mean of that observation's nonmissing values for items on the scale in place of item responses on that scale that are missing.

A major advantage of individual mean substitution is that all nonmissing information on items within a scale for the given individual is used in the estimation of the missing values. However, this approach presumes that the items having missing values are similar in difficulty or extremity to items with nonmissing values. If the items having missing values are extreme in some sense and thus should generate more extreme answers, substituting the mean for less extreme items would bias the characterization of any participant with missing values.

Regression Substitution

A researcher can use regression analysis to produce a predicted score on a given variable using information from other variables. Suppose that missing values are present for some participants on variable Y, but that complete data are available from all participants on variables X_1–X_p. One could then regress Y on variables X_1–X_p using data from persons having nonmissing data on Y. Then, for persons with missing data on Y, one could substitute the predicted Y score based on the regression equation for their missing Y value.

51

Regression substitution has one major strength—the substituted values are consistent with specified relations among variables in the data set. But, this strength is accompanied by an important weakness—the predicted values are "too good," or too consistent with the analytic model. In most areas of developmental psychology, squared multiple correlations are in the range from .20–.50, consistent with a considerable amount of variability of obtained scores about any regression line. Because regression substitution involves using substitute values that fall directly on the regression line, the method will lead to positively biased estimates of the strength of relation of predictors with a criterion.

Single Imputation

In single imputation, a single data set with nonmissing values for all observations on all variables is produced from the original data set that contains missing values. Conceptually, imputation proceeds by developing initial estimates for all missing values that are maximally consistent with the multivariate trends in all data included in the imputation step (as done in regression substitution), but then adds some stochastic or random variability to these substitute values so that the data will mimic the uncertainty in relations among variables present in the nonmissing values. Thus, in any analysis, imputed values should show comparable lack of fit or residual variability as exhibited by nonmissing values.

The major strength of single imputation is that a researcher has a single, complete data set on which all analyses can be performed. This greatly simplifies all analyses, as the same sample size is used in all analyses, and only a single set of results needs to be described and interpreted. Because no observations are deleted from the data set, single imputation maximizes power by retaining all participants in analyses. Furthermore, the data set will exhibit all trends that were present in the nonmissing values, including reasonable levels of lack of fit of models to data.

One potential weakness concerns the representativeness of the single data set that is the outcome of the imputation step. Because a stochastic, random component is added to each imputed value and these random components would not be repeated exactly if the imputation process were repeated, any single imputed data set may contain unusual imputations. The solution to this problem is to perform multiple imputations (see as follows). A second potential weakness involves the selection of variables included in the imputation step. If interactive or nonlinear effects of variables are present in the nonmissing values in the original data set, then appropriate product or powered terms must be included in the imputation process or else the interactive or nonlinear effects will not be exhibited by the imputed values. Hence, imputation requires that the analyst have an accurate idea about the types of relations among variables that are expected for the imputation process to capture the true trends in the data.

Multiple Imputation

Multiple imputation, as the name implies, is the extension of simple imputation to the construction of multiple "complete" data sets with imputed values. In each of the multiple "complete" data sets, all nonmissing values from the original data set are identical across data sets. But the imputed values developed to replace missing values will differ across complete data sets. That is, because a stochastic, random component is part of each imputed value and the stochastic component is a draw from a random process, the imputed value for a given observation for a particular variable will differ from one complete data set to another.

Multiple imputation has all of the strengths of single imputation, so these need not be reiterated here. In addition, multiple imputation resolves the representativeness problem associated with single imputation because the multiple complete data sets will converge on full representativeness as the number of data sets imputed increases. Multiple imputation remains subject to the potential problem of nonlinear and interactive effects of variables, necessitating the inclusion of all such potential effects in the imputation model. One other difficulty associated with multiple imputation is the need to summarize information on parameter estimates across the multiple samples. Experts typically recommend that between 5 and 10 complete data sets be constructed. Then, each individual analysis must be performed in each of the multiply imputed data sets, and parameters and their standard errors (*SEs*) must be based on a summary of the individual estimates and their *SEs* in the multiple samples. Performing such summaries is more tedious and potentially error prone than difficult, but the increase in effort can be substantial if a large number of analyses are conducted.

Direct Fitting

Direct fitting is a term signifying the fitting of a model directly to the raw data for each observation. Direct fitting goes by several names, including the increasingly familiar full information maximum likelihood, or FIML, estimation. In the presence of missing data, FIML estimation involves the fitting of the model to the nonmissing values for each observation, ignoring the presence of missing values.

53

FIML estimation has virtually all of the strengths of single or multiple imputation. Akin to single imputation, only a single data set is analyzed, easing the analytic burden. Furthermore, no imputation step must be taken, as the imputation process is implicit—contained within the fitting of the model to the data.

The principal weakness of FIML estimation is the need to ensure that all variables related to missingness on key analysis variables are themselves included in the analysis. If one fails to include in an analysis all variables related to missingness on the central outcome variables, resulting parameter estimates will be biased.

IMPLICATIONS AND RECOMMENDATIONS REGARDING HANDLING MISSING DATA

What Difference Does It Make?

After discussing the various ways of handling missing data, researchers might want to know how much all of this really matters. To investigate this issue, I simulated data for 120 participants in a simple research situation involving two variables X and Y, with a moderate, positive, linear relation specified between X and Y. All analyses were performed using LISREL 8 (Jöreskog & Sörbom, 1996). For estimating parameters from population data, I used the population means, SDs, and correlation matrix as input data and specified that sample size was 120, to obtain estimates of parameters and their SEs as if only a limited sample size of 120 participants were available. For sample analyses of complete data, I used the sample means, SDs, and correlation matrix from the 120 simulated participants. Next, I deleted one-third of the observed values on Y in two different ways, as described as follows. Then, I used five methods for handling missing data: listwise deletion, pairwise deletion, mean substitution, regression substitution, and direct fitting (i.e., FIML estimation). For the first four of these methods, I used the given method to estimate missing data, then computed the sample statistics (means, SDs, and correlation matrix), and used sample statistics as input data. For FIML estimation, I used LISREL to fit models directly to the raw data, with a missing data flag (-9) inserted in place of missing values on Y.

Complete Data

The population parameters for the mean and SD on X and Y and for the correlation between X and Y are shown in the first data line in the top section of Table 1, along with SEs of the population parameters based on a sample

TABLE 1

BASIC STATISTICS FOR TWO-VARIABLE PROBLEM UNDER DIFFERENT METHODS OF TREATING MISSING DATA

Data	N	X Mean	X SD	Y Mean	Y SD	Correlation
Complete data						
Population	120	10.00 (.18)	2.00 (.13)	5.00 (.09)	1.00 (.07)	.50 (.07)
Sample	120	9.85 (.20)	2.16 (.14)	4.92 (.10)	1.12 (.07)	.52 (.07)
Missing completely at random (MCAR)						
Listwise deletion	80	9.77 (.26)	2.29 (.18)	4.86 (.13)	1.11 (.09)	.54 (.08)
Pairwise deletion	80(?)	9.85 (.20)	2.16 (.14)	4.86 (.10)	1.11 (.07)	.57 (.06)
Mean substitution	120	9.85 (.20)	2.16 (.14)	4.86 (.08)	.91 (.06)	.47 (.07)
Regression substitution	120	9.85 (.20)	2.16 (.14)	4.88 (.09)	.95 (.06)	.60 (.06)
Direct fit (FIML)	120	9.85 (.20)	2.15 (.14)	4.88 (.12)	1.09 (.09)	.52 (.08)
Missing at random (MAR)						
Listwise deletion	80	11.00 (.17)	1.49 (.12)	5.22 (.12)	1.02 (.08)	.39 (.10)
Pairwise deletion	80(?)	9.85 (.20)	2.16 (.14)	5.22 (.09)	1.02 (.07)	.27 (.09)
Mean substitution	120	9.85 (.20)	2.16 (.14)	5.22 (.08)	.83 (.05)	.22 (.09)
Regression substitution	120	9.85 (.20)	2.16 (.14)	4.92 (.09)	.96 (.06)	.60 (.06)
Direct fit (FIML)	120	9.85 (.20)	2.15 (.14)	4.92 (.12)	1.09 (.09)	.52 (.08)

Note.—Tabled values are parameter estimates, with standard errors in parentheses. Sample size for pairwise deletion is listed as 80(?) because three sample estimates (mean and *SD* of *Y*, correlation between *X* and *Y*) are based on 80 observations, but two sample estimates (mean and *SD* of *X*) are based on 120 observations.

size of 120. Immediately below the population parameters are sample estimates of the population parameters based on the sample of 120 simulated participants. Inspection of Table 1 shows that the simulated sample leads to sample statistics that closely mirror the population parameters. For example, the sample mean and *SD* on *X* of 9.85 and 2.16, respectively, were close to the population parameters of 10.0 and 2.0, respectively, and the sample correlation between *X* and *Y* of $r = .52$ was close to the population parameter of $\rho = .50$.

If one employs the same data to perform a simple linear regression analysis predicting *Y* from *X*, results are as shown in the top two lines in Table 2. The population intercept and raw score regression coefficient *B* were 2.50 and .25, respectively, residual variance was .75, and the squared multiple *R* was .25. Using the complete data from the sample of 120 simulated participants, the intercept and *B* values were 2.29 and .27, respectively, residual variance was .92, and the squared multiple *R* was .27, all relatively close to the respective population values.

TABLE 2

REGRESSION RESULTS FOR TWO-VARIABLE PROBLEM UNDER DIFFERENT METHODS OF
TREATING MISSING DATA

| | | Regression Equation | | Residual | |
Data	N	Intercept	B	Variance	R^2
Complete Data					
Population	120	2.50 (.41)	.25 (.04)	.75 (.10)	.25
Sample	120	2.29 (.41)	.27 (.04)	.92 (.12)	.27
Missing completely at random (MCAR)					
Listwise deletion	80	2.28 (.46)	.26 (.05)	.88 (.14)	.29
Pairwise deletion	80(?)	1.95 (.40)	.30 (.04)	.83 (.10)	.33
Mean substitution	120	2.93 (.34)	.20 (.03)	.64 (.08)	.22
Regression substitution	120	2.28 (.33)	.26 (.03)	.58 (.08)	.36
Direct fit (FIML)	120	2.28 (.49)	.26 (.05)	.86 (.14)	.27
Missing at random (MAR)					
Listwise deletion	80	2.33 (.78)	.26 (.07)	.89(.14)	.15
Pairwise deletion	80(?)	3.99 (.42)	.13 (.04)	.97 (.13)	.07
Mean substitution	120	4.40 (.35)	.08 (.03)	.66 (.09)	.05
Regression substitution	120	2.33 (.33)	.26 (.03)	.59 (.08)	.36
Direct fit (FIML)	120	2.33 (.49)	.26 (.05)	.88 (.14)	.27

Note.—Tabled values are parameter estimates, with standard errors in parentheses. Sample size for pairwise deletion is listed as 80(?) because three sample estimates (mean and *SD* of *Y*, correlation between *X* and *Y*) are based on 80 observations, but two sample estimates (mean and *SD* of *X*) are based on 120 observations.

Simulation 1: MCAR Data

To obtain MCAR data, I randomly deleted 40 of the 120 values on *Y*, without any consideration of the magnitude of the *X* or *Y* values. The scatterplot of *Y* on *X* for the complete sample of 120 participants is shown in Figure 1A, and the scatterplot on the restricted sample of 80 participants with MCAR data on *Y* is shown in Figure 1B. Inspection of these two figures reveals that the scatterplot in Figure 1B appears to be simply a less dense, but highly similar sampling of points as that shown in Figure 1A, with similar means and ranges of scores on *X* and *Y* across the two graphs.

Estimates of means and *SD*s on *X* and *Y* and the correlation between *X* and *Y* are shown in the middle section of Table 1 for the five methods of

FIGURE 1.—Scatterplot and least-squares regression line for (A) complete data set for simulated participants ($N = 120$), (B) Missing completely at random (MCAR) data set for which values on *Y* were deleted randomly for one-third of simulated participants ($N = 80$), and (C) Missing at random (MAR) data set for which values on *Y* were deleted for the one-third of participants with lowest scores on *X* ($N = 80$).

A

Complete Data On Y
Y = 2.29 + 0.26 X + e

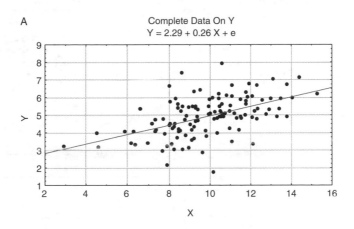

B

33% Y MCAR

Y = 2.28 + 0.26 X + e

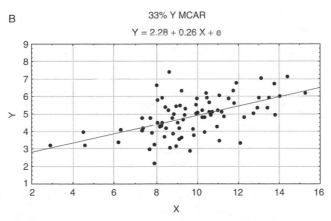

C

33% Y MAR (Y missing for smallest X)

Y = 2.33 + 0.26 X + e

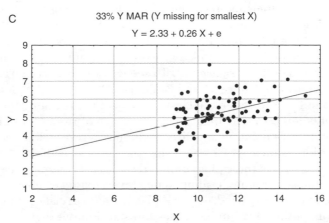

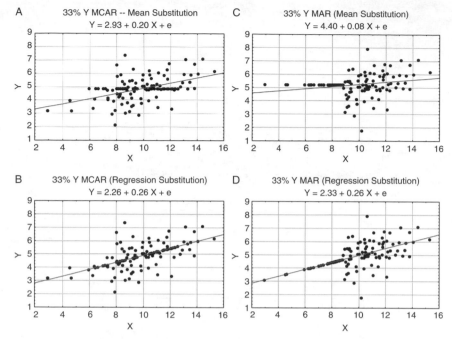

FIGURE 2.—Scatterplot and least squares regression line for simulated participants ($N = 120$) with (A) Missing completely at random (MCAR) missing values on Y replaced by the sample mean on Y or (B) a regression estimate derived from analysis of data for the 80 participants with complete data on X and Y, or (C) Missing at random (MAR) missing values on Y replaced by the sample mean on Y or (D) a regression estimate derived from analysis of data for the 80 participants with complete data on X and Y.

handling missing data. Under listwise deletion, all data for the 40 participants with missing values on Y were deleted, so the mean and SD on both X and Y differ from their sample values. For all remaining methods, all 120 values on X were used in calculations, so all methods reproduced the sample values well. All five methods yielded close estimates of the mean of Y, although mean substitution and regression substitution led to negatively biased estimates of the variance of Y. To see why this occurred, refer to the scatterplots shown in Figure 2A and B. Figure 2A contains the plot in which missing values on Y were replaced by the mean of Y, accounting for the large number of points on a horizontal line at the mean of Y (4.86). In Figure 2B, we see a buildup of points falling directly on the regression line, as these are the regression estimates of Y values for participants with MCAR missing values on Y. In both of these plots, imputed values fall closer to the mean of Y than do nonmissing values, leading to negatively biased estimates of the SD of Y. Note also the expected negative bias in the correlation under mean substitution, positive bias under regression substitution, slight positive bias under listwise or pairwise deletion, and precise estimation of the correlation under FIML estimation.

Regression results for these data are shown in the middle section of Table 2. When compared against the estimates from the complete sample that are shown in the top section of Table 2, the two missing data methods that provide similar estimates of all parameters and SEs are listwise deletion and FIML. Both of these methods yield good, essentially equivalent estimates of the intercept, slope B, residual variance, and R^2 parameters; FIML had a slightly positively biased SE for the intercept, and listwise deletion a slight positive bias in the R^2. The remaining methods had more serious problems: (a) pairwise deletion, with negative bias in intercept and positive bias in slope and R^2; (b) mean substitution, with positive bias in intercept and negative bias in slope, residual variance, and R^2; and (c) regression substitution, with stronger negative bias in residual variance and positive bias in R^2. Clearly, the best methods were listwise deletion and FIML, with FIML having a slight edge due to accurate representation of the R^2 value.

Simulation 2: MAR Data

Next, I returned to the complete set of simulated data and deleted the Y values for the 40 observations with the smallest values on X. Clearly, the probability of missingness on Y is highly and directly related to X, but this should not be a problem for a modern method of handling missing data if X is included in analyses. In fact, this type of data structure is likely to be encountered in many applied situations. For example, assume that X is high school GPA and Y is first-year college GPA from a highly selective college, and the 120 participants constitute the applicants for admission to the college. Then, the 80 participants with nonmissing values on Y are the applicants selected for admission who matriculated at the college and had first-year college GPAs, whereas the 40 participants with missing values on first-year college GPA were those applicants turned down for admission.

The scatterplot of the data for the 80 participants with nonmissing values on Y is shown in Figure 1c. When Figure 1c is compared against Figure 1A, it is clear that the only persons retained in the MAR data set are the two-thirds of participants with the highest scores on X. As a result, the means on both X and Y in Figure 1c are higher than in Figure 1A, and the ranges of values on X and Y are greatly restricted. Because of this, the listwise deletion analyses, which are shown in the bottom section of Table 1, led to positive bias in the estimates of the means of X and Y, negative bias in the estimated SDs, and negative bias in the R^2 due to restriction of range on X. Pairwise deletion and mean substitution results in accurate estimation of mean and SD of X, but positive bias in the estimate of the mean of Y and negative bias in both the estimates of *SD* of *Y* and the correlation between *X* and *Y*. Regression substitution led to fairly good estimates of most parameters, but negatively biased estimate of *SD* of *Y* and positive bias in the correlation between *X* and *Y*. In contrast, FIML estimation led to very accurate estimation of all parameters, especially the correlation between *X* and *Y*.

Regression results for the MAR data set are shown in the bottom section of Table 2. Listwise deletion provided reasonable representation of most parameters except for a highly inflated estimate of the *SE* for the intercept and an R^2 value that was about half the correct value (.15 vs. .27). Both pairwise deletion and mean substitution led to rather poor estimates of all parameters, with particularly poor, negatively biased estimates of the strength of the relation between *X* and *Y*, as reflected in the R^2 values of .07 and .05, respectively. Regression substitution led to good recovery of the intercept and slope, but once again had notable negative bias in estimation of residual variance and positive bias in the estimated R^2. The basis for the negative bias in the R^2 under mean substitution and the positive bias under regression substitution can be seen by inspecting the scatterplots in Figure 4C and 4D. Under mean substitution, the imputed values are shown along a horizontal line at 5.22, falling far from the true regression line and severely attenuating the estimated relation between *X* and *Y*. In contrast, the imputed values under regression substitution fall directly on the regression line, failing to exhibit any residual variability and thereby inflating the R^2 and leading to severe underestimation of overall residual variance. Finally, FIML estimation again performed in stellar fashion, with accurate estimates of intercept, slope, residual variance, and R^2, and reasonable, if slightly positively biased, estimates of the *SE*s of the parameters.

Comments

Because of space limitations, I was unable to include analyses using multiple imputation, but multiple imputation should have performed identically to FIML with the simulated data sets. Also, among the five methods used in this small study, FIML estimation was the only method that performed adequately for both the MCAR and MAR data sets.

Recommendations

Given the potential bias that can arise when using nonoptimal methods of handling missing data, I provide a number of recommendations here that I consider most crucial. Interested readers should consult the recommended sources listed at the end of this section to obtain a complete list of recommendations regarding handling of missing data.

Analysis recommendation 1: Perform initial descriptive analyses of data to identify the nature and extent of missing data. This recommendation is a common one with regard to data analysis and consists mainly of stating that a researcher should *know* his or her data. But, because optimal ways of dealing with missing data may hinge on the amount of missing data, this frequent recommendation has greater urgency.

Analysis recommendation 2: When item nonresponse on scales is relatively minor, consider using single imputation or substitution. If the missing data in a data set consists only of occasional item nonresponse and the incidence of such item nonresponse is relatively minor (e.g., 1% or 2% of the entries in the data set), a researcher should consider using a single imputation or some method of substitution. Very minor levels of missing data will lead to essentially identical results across different methods of missing data, and the detrimental effects of using sample mean or individual mean substitution will not occur because of the small number of missing values. Because many individuals might have one or two missing item responses, listwise deletion is not recommended, as too many observations would be deleted. If item nonresponse occurs at some higher level (8–10% or more) but no scale nonresponse occurs, then a single imputation might be in order.

Analysis recommendation 3: If the amount of missing data in the entire data set is very small, consider using single imputation. If missing data consist of item nonresponse, scale nonresponse, or drop-out, but the level of missing data is low, then a single imputation may be sufficient. No hard and fast rules can be generated with regard to what constitutes low, moderate, and high levels of missing data. But, 1–2% missing is rather low, levels of 10–15% or higher seem moderate, and levels of 25% or higher are relatively high. But, experts on missing data often claim that missingness on any individual variable can be 50% or higher and optimal methods (i.e., imputation or FIML) will handle the analyses quite well (Graham & Schafer, 1999; McArdle, 1994). Now, if missing data are at a low level, a single imputation is probably in order, as the problem of missing data is so minor that the benefits associated with multiple imputation are likely not worth the additional effort.

Analysis recommendation 4: If the amount of missing data is moderate or large and the variables related to missingness cannot be included in all analyses, use multiple imputation. This recommendation is relatively straightforward: in the presence of moderate or large amounts of missing data, multiple imputation is a very reasonable alternative, particularly if one cannot assure that variables related to missingness will be included in all analytic models. Multiple imputation is especially well suited to longitudinal investigations with many variables because the investigator may be unsure about which variables are related to missingness on which other variables. The solution to this dilemma is to include a large and expansive set of variables in the imputation step so that any variable that is potentially related to missingness on any key variable has its effects represented during the imputation process. Then, in later analyses, the researcher can be less concerned about whether variables related to missingness of outcome variables are included in any particular analysis because these missingness-related variables were included in the imputation stage and their effects were therefore included in the imputed values. If this is the tack taken with a data set, researchers should be sure to include product and powered variables representing predicted interaction and nonlinear effects in the imputation step because failure to include such information in imputation will tend to wash out these effects in the imputed data sets.

Analysis Recommendation 5: If the amount of missing data is moderate or large, but variables related to missingness can be included in analytic models, consider using FIML estimation. In many longitudinal investigations, attrition is related to variables assessed at the first time of measurement. For example, in studies of ability development, participants who drop-out at some point after the first time of measurement tend to score lower initially on ability variables. If longitudinal trends in ability are the object of analysis, inclusion of the Time 1 scores on variables within the model will control for missingness on these same variables at later times of measurement. So, variables directly related to missingness are included in the analytic model, and FIML estimation should be used on a data set that includes all participants regardless of whether they participated in only one occasion of measurement.

Professional recommendation 1: Use modern methods of handling missing data—imputation or FIML—in your research, or at least do not denigrate those who do. I recently reviewed a manuscript submitted for review to *Child Development* that used imputation. The authors had a sample of moderate size ($N = 60$), had some missing data, so used imputation methods. I applauded the use of these methods in my review, but at least one other reviewer felt the authors were making up data through imputation. This reviewer recommended that the authors use listwise deletion to pare the sample down to only those observations with complete data on all variables and then base all analyses on this reduced sample. This amounts to asking the authors to perform analyses in a biased fashion with even less power because observations with missing values would be dropped. Authors and reviewers should become acquainted with modern methods of handling missing data so improper suggestions of this sort will not be made.

Professional recommendation 2: Integrate courses on missing data into your curricula. Given the ubiquity of missing data in longitudinal studies, the lack of classes or portions of classes in our standard curricula that deal with problems and solutions related to missing data is unfortunate. In advanced classes, such as those that cover structural equation modeling, students often receive an introduction to analytic methods for handling missing data, but greater integration of these methods into our curricula should be afforded in the future. Faculty members should encourage the development of one or more graduate classes dealing with missing data to ensure that students are exposed to state-of-the-art procedures on this crucial issue.

Professional recommendation 3: Find out about methods of dealing with missing data. Perhaps the best way of acquainting yourself with new methods for handling data is to read recent papers or books on the topic, and I offer here a few of my favorites. Schafer and Graham (2002) gave a very thorough and readable review of state-of-the-art techniques, and their recommendations are largely consistent with those of the current chapter. Another very readable review was published recently by Acock (2005), and Collins, Schafer, and Kam (2001) presented an informative simulation study of different missing data approaches that demonstrates clearly their strengths and weaknesses in representing trends in data. As for monograph or book-length treatments, Allison (2002) gives an understandable, introductory presentation of virtually all issues that should be considered, and the books by Little and Rubin (2002) and Schafer (1997) provide more technical but more complete coverage of the field. Finally, Acock (2005) and Schafer and Graham (2002) give good summaries of statistical software that can be used to perform analyses related to the missing data solutions discussed previously.

ACKNOWLEDGMENTS

Support for this work was provided by grants from the National Institute on Drug Abuse and the National Institute on Alcohol Abuse and Alcoholism (DA017902) and from the National Institute of Mental Health (MH051361).

I would like to thank the series editors, the volume editors, and the anonymous reviewers for helpful comments on a prior draft of this chapter.

REFERENCES

Acock, A. C. (2005). Working with missing data. *Journal of Marriage and Family*, **67**, 1012–1028.

Allison, P. D. (2002). *Missing data*. Thousand Oaks, CA: Sage.

Bakeman, R. (2006). The practical importance of findings. In K. McCartney & M. Burchinal (Eds.), *Best practices in developmental research. Monographs for the Society for Research in Child Development* **71** (13).

Burchinal, M., & Appelbaum, M. I. (1991). Estimating individual developmental functions: Methods and their assumptions. *Child Development*, **62**, 23–43.

Collins, L. M. (2006). Analysis of longitudinal data: The integration of theoretical model, temporal design, and statistical method. *Annual Review of Psychology*, **57**, 505–528.

Collins, L. M., Schafer, J. L., & Kam, C.-M. (2001). A comparison of inclusive and restrictive strategies in modern missing data procedures. *Psychological Methods*, **6**, 330–351.

Ferrer, E., Salthouse, T. A., McArdle, J. J., Stewart, W. F., & Schwartz, B. S. (2005). Multivariate modeling of age and retest in longitudinal studies of cognitive abilities. *Psychology and Aging*, **20**, 412–422.

Ferrer, E., Salthouse, T. A., Stewart, W. F., & Schwartz, B. S. (2004). Modeling age and retest processes in longitudinal studies of cognitive abilities. *Psychology and Aging*, **19**, 243–259.

Gollob, H. F., & Reichardt, C. S. (1987). Taking account of time lags in causal models. *Child Development*, **58**, 80–92.

Graham, J. W., & Schafer, J. L. (1999). On the performance of multiple imputation for multivariate data with small sample size. In R. Hoyle (Ed.), *Statistical strategies for small sample research* (pp. 1–29). Thousand Oaks, CA: Sage.

Jöreskog, K. G., & Sörbom, D. (1996). *LISREL 8 user's reference guide [computer software manual]*. Mooresville, IN: Scientific Software Inc.

Levin, B. E., Katzen, H. L., Klein, B., & Llabre, M. L. (2000). Cognitive decline affects subject attrition in longitudinal research. *Journal of Clinical and Experimental Neuropsychology*, **22**, 580–586.

Little, R. J. A., & Rubin, D. B. (1987). *Statistical analysis with missing data*. New York: Wiley.

Little, R. J. A., & Rubin, D. B. (2002). *Statistical analysis with missing data* (2nd ed.). New York: Wiley.

McArdle, J. J. (1994). Structural factor analysis experiments with incomplete data. *Multivariate Behavioral Research*, **29**, 409–454.

McArdle, J. J., & Epstein, D. (1987). Latent growth curves within developmental structural equation models. *Child Development*, **58**, 110–133.

McArdle, J. J., & Hamagami, F. (1991). Modeling incomplete longitudinal and cross-sectional data using latent growth structural models. In L. M. Collins & J. L. Horn (Eds.), *Best methods for the analysis of change* (pp. 276–304). Washington, DC: American Psychological Association.

McArdle, J. J., & Woodcock, R. W. (1997). Expanding test–retest designs to include developmental time-lag components. *Psychological Methods*, **2**, 403–435.

Nesselroade, J. R., & Baltes, P. B. (1974). Adolescent personality development and historical change: 1970–1972. *Monographs of the Society for Research in Child Development*, **39** (1, Serial No. 154).

Rubin, D. B. (1976). Inference and missing data. *Biometrika*, **63**, 581–592.

Rubin, D. B. (1987). *Multiple imputation for nonresponse in surveys*. New York: Wiley.

Schafer, J. L. (1997). *Analysis of incomplete multivariate data*. London: Chapman and Hall.

Schafer, J. L., & Graham, J. W. (2002). Missing data: Our view of the state of the art. *Psychological Methods*, **7**, 147–177.

Siddiqui, O., Flay, B. R., & Hu, F. B. (1996). Factors affecting attrition in a longitudinal smoking prevention study. *Preventive Medicine*, **25**, 554–560.

IV. GROWTH CURVE ANALYSIS: AN INTRODUCTION TO VARIOUS METHODS FOR ANALYZING LONGITUDINAL DATA

Methods for analyzing longitudinal data provide researchers with powerful tools for describing developmental patterns and identifying predictors of development. A wide variety of analytic methods are available for describing developmental patterns and identifying predictors of development. The purpose of this chapter is to provide an overview of five of the currently available analytic approaches to estimate growth curves for continuous outcomes. We focus on describing the assumptions and outline the limitations a researcher faces when using univariate and multivariate repeated measures analysis of variance, hierarchical linear models (HLM), latent growth curve models (LGC), and prototypic or growth mixture model methods. Using a simulated data set and data from a child care intervention study, we demonstrate the strengths and weaknesses of each approach.

Data analysis for developmental projects provides the mechanism for testing the research questions with project data. Ideally, statistical analysis integrates the three elements of a longitudinal study: theoretical model of change, longitudinal design, and statistical models (Burchinal & Appelbaum, 1991; Collins, 2006; Singer & Willett, 2003). The project should be based on a well-articulated theory of change that dictated the study design to ensure that data collection adequately capture the hypothesized change and processes implicated in that theory (Collins, 2006). Selection of the analytic methods follows logically in a well-designed study based on a clearly articulated theory of change.

A wide variety of analytic methods are readily available, but not all researchers know how to select a method that matches both their theory of change and the data they collected. The purpose of this chapter is to provide an overview of some of the currently available analytic approaches to estimating growth curves. We limit this presentation to methods for continuous outcomes, although there are a whole class of methods that address questions about when events occur (see Singer & Willett, 2003, for an introduction to survival analysis), predictors of discrete events over time (see Diggle, Liang, & Zeger, 1994, for an introduction to generalized estimating equations and longitudinal logistic regression), or transition over time in latent class membership (see Clogg, 1995; Collins, 2006, for a discussion of latent class analysis methods).

GOALS OF LONGITUDINAL ANALYSES

The primary goal of longitudinal analysis of repeated measures and growth curve analyses in particular is to describe patterns of change over time. We would like to chart individual developmental patterns. Ideally, we would like to describe the underlying developmental trajectory (Burchinal & Appelbaum, 1991; Blanton & Jaccard, 2006). This trajectory provides the mathematical description of the development of a given attribute over time. The trajectory specifies the type of equation or form of the developmental trajectory, and is uniquely defined for a given person by that individual's parameters. Nonlinear functions such as exponential or logistic functions have been very useful because they describe change that is very rapid at first and then slows down until the final level is reached and growth stops (Willett, Singer, & Martin, 1997; Vonesh, 1996). The parameters of that trajectory describe important characteristics of growth such as the age at which the growth spurt starts, the rate of change during the growth spurt, and the final level of the attribute at the end of the growth spurt. Other functions, such as polynomial growth curves, provide reasonable descriptions of growth and are especially useful when our measurement of the underlying attribute is not precise or when relatively few repeated assessments were collected (Singer & Willett, 2003). These functions have parameters that describe the initial or mean level of the attribute, rate of linear change over time, and rates of higher order patterns of change (e.g., quadratic, cubic, etc.). Higher order polynomial growth curves can describe growth patterns in which the rate of change is not constant over time.

For example, height is an attribute with a developmental trajectory that is well described. We can measure height accurately on a ratio scale, and our measurement reflects exactly how tall the individual is at that time. We know that changes in height over time can be well described with a series of linked nonlinear functions (Bock, Wainer, Peterson, Thissen, Jurray, & Roch, 1973). The first three-parameter logistic nonlinear trajectory describes the infant growth spurt between birth and 3 years of age. Growth is very rapid during early infancy and slows as the child approaches his or her third birthday. Growth tends to be linear between the end of the infant growth spurt and the beginning of the adolescent growth spurt. The adolescent growth spurt is well described, again, by a three-parameter logistic nonlinear function. Children tend to follow the same growth pattern, so population curves have been estimated and are used by pediatricians as an index of well-child development, to determine whether a given child seems to be growing as expected, and also to compare groups of individuals or identify predictors of developmental patterns.

In addition to describing development, we want to identify predictors of patterns of change. We would like to know what personal, family, school, or community characteristics are related to individual developmental patterns. Are there differences between groups in terms of rate of change or level of development? Are there characteristics of the individual, schools or employment, family, or community that predict developmental trajectories? For example, if you were studying height, you might want to know if smaller children at birth show a bigger growth spurt during infancy.

LIMITING FACTORS IN DESCRIBING PATTERNS OF CHANGE

Our ability to measure the outcome often limits the extent to which we can describe patterns of change. It is far more difficult to describe development of many psychological attributes other than height because they cannot be measured as accurately as height or weight (Blanton & Jaccard, 2006). We have good instruments for measuring characteristics such as language, intelligence, academic achievement, behavior problems, and prosocial skills. These measures have good reliability and reasonable validity, but they provide approximate, not exact or isomorphic, assessments of the trait. When measurement is approximate, we can meaningfully describe individual differences in developmental patterns based on norm-referenced or criterion-referenced assessments even when we cannot describe the underlying developmental trajectory accurately. Growth curve analyses on instruments that provide approximate, not exact, measurement can tell us a great deal about both intra-individual developmental trajectories and inter-individual differences in patterns of change.

Sample size and number of repeated assessments often limit our ability to describe individual patterns of change. Most longitudinal research includes relatively few repeated measures on most individuals and modest to moderate sample sizes. The accuracy of our statistical model to describe an individual's data is extremely limited when there are only a few repeated assessments. Similarly, our ability to identify individual differences is limited when our samples are small. Longitudinal research is expensive and humans tend to grow slowly, so it is very costly to collect large numbers of repeated assessments on large samples. Statistical methods vary in their ability to provide precise and valid test statistics when fit to short time series or with small samples. Accelerated longitudinal designs (i.e., designs in which multiple cohorts are observed for shorter periods of time allow for describing growth across all ages accessed) can provide efficient means to describe developmental patterns even with relatively few assessments per individual (see Graham, Taylor, & Cumsville, 2001 for details).

Finally, any longitudinal method must account for correlations among repeated measures. Almost all repeated assessments of humans are correlated because skill levels at one time are correlated with skill levels at other times. It is this dependency that is being modeled when we estimate the developmental trajectory. Failure to adequately account for these correlations often renders test statistics invalid because variability is often underestimated, resulting in overestimating statistics (Tabachnick & Fidell, 2007). When that happens, p-values as an index of whether associations between predictors and developmental patterns are not statistically valid. Longitudinal methods vary markedly in their ability to appropriately account for correlations in repeated measures.

STATISTICAL ASSUMPTIONS FOR LONGITUDINAL MODELS

Most statistical methods for testing hypotheses share a common set of assumptions that need to be met when analyzing both cross-sectional and longitudinal data (Tabachnick & Fidell, 2007). These assumptions are presented and then many of them are discussed in the context of specific methods for analyzing longitudinal data. The mostly commonly used cross-sectional and longitudinal methods assume that the developmental outcome variables are normally distributed and measured at the interval or ratio level; they may also be a transformation of those variables that is normally distributed. This assumption can be relaxed somewhat, but variables need to have roughly symmetric, unimodal distributions in which more data are in the middle of the distribution than at either end of the distribution. The scale of measurement can be ordinal as long as there are at least four levels represented within the data and the distribution is roughly normal (Gebotys, 1993). Parameter coefficients cannot be trusted to describe population tendencies when the outcome has a distribution that is markedly skewed or when very few distinct levels are represented in the data. A wide variety of methods also exist for analyzing data with other distributions but require more specialized techniques (e.g., autoregressive models to examine stability and change, poison regression for count data, exponential or logistic methods for nonlinear data, censored models for data with a large number of values at the minimum value; see McArdle & Nesselroade, 2003, for details). Similarly, most longitudinal methods require an appropriate between-subjects model that includes relevant main effects and interactions (Tabachnick & Fidell, 2007). The model coefficients are biased when important covariates or interactions are omitted. Finally, it is also assumed that at some level in the data there are independent units of observations. The test-statistics' p-values are usually too small when independence of observations is falsely assumed. The consequence of violating any of these assumptions is that test statistics are not valid and cannot be trusted to indicate whether predictors relate to patterns of change.

Several additional assumptions must also be met when repeated measures are analyzed with methods that test hypotheses about change over time. First, it is assumed that you have specified a longitudinal model that can adequately describe change over time for individuals (see Burchinal & Appelbaum, 1991 or Singer & Willett, 2003, for more detail), but the type and level of that model is limited by the number of repeated assessments in several ways. With two repeated assessments, we can only estimate a separate intercept or slope for each individual, but not both (note: while some methodologists such as Rogosa, Brandt, & Willett, 1982, argue that you must have more than two repeated assessments to use longitudinal methods, all argue that you must take the correlation among repeated measures even with two assessments). With three repeated measures we typically estimate an individual linear growth curve, with a separate intercept and slope that describe rate of change with respect to time or age for each individual. With four repeated assessments, we can choose between nonlinear functions with three parameters such as the exponential growth curve or the quadratic polynomial function. For example, the three-parameter exponential function describes monotonically increasing change as a function time of onset of growth spurt, maximum rate of change, and a final, or asymptotic, level. In contrast, the quadratic polynomial function describes change as a function of level, linear change, and quadratic change, and it estimates a parabolic function. With five or more repeated assessments, we can fit nonlinear functions such as logistic growth curves or higher order polynomial functions such as cubic growth curves. These functions can describe change that is S shaped. Thus, it is important to have enough repeated assessments to permit the estimation of hypothesized individual growth curves.

It is imperative that the selected growth curve model accounts for the pattern of correlations within repeated assessments to rely on the test statistics to identify predictors of developmental patterns (Singer & Willett, 2003). A model will completely account for these correlations if the number of parameters estimated is one less than the number of repeated assessments. On the other hand, a model with substantially fewer parameters than repeated assessments will provide more power for hypothesis testing, assuming the model accurately describes developmental change. We offer a couple of recommendations to balance power and model adequacy based on our years of statistical experience. First, when the number of repeated measures is three or fewer, we recommend that the number of parameters in the initial individual growth curve model be close to one minus the number of repeated measures. Second, when the number of repeated measures is four or greater, we suggest fitting a preliminary model that is at least one degree higher than the hypothesized polynomial growth curve model to test whether the hypothesized model is adequate. For example, if one believes change is approximately quadratic and there are at least four repeated measures, then you can fit a cubic model in a preliminary analysis. If the random variance and associated covariances for the cubic term are inestimable or nonsignificant, then you should refit the model as a quadratic model.

A related issue that must be addressed is deciding whether the population and individual growth curves have the same or different growth curve models. Typically, the same type of growth curve model is estimated to describe both individual and group patterns of change, but this is not necessary or even desirable in all cases. The individual growth curve parameters describe the extent to which that individual differs from the population for that index of change (e.g., mean level, slope), whereas the group growth curve parameters describe the overall shape of the population curve. Therefore, individual differences can be relatively minor for higher order terms in a polynomial model even when the group-level parameter is clearly needed to describe patterns of change. In this case, omitting the higher order term from the group model would bias all of the other parameter estimates, but including this term in the individual model decreases power and often may result in a model that cannot be estimated. Although uncommon in psychology, use of different individual and group growth curve models is a common approach in biostatistics. A leading statistician demonstrated that blood pressure can be characterized by a quadratic group curve and a linear individual curve because the overall shape of the curve was quadratic and there were marked individual differences in both the intercept and slope (Laird & Ware, 1982). Conversely, it is possible that substantial individual differences exist for higher order polynomial terms, but those terms average to zero. In that case, the population curve would not show that level of curvature even though individual growth curves would. In developmental psychology, Burchinal, Campbell, Bryant, Wasik, and Ramey (1997) published an example of the use of a quadratic group growth curve model and a linear individual growth curve model. The individuals had at least three repeated assessments and the developmental pattern was quadratic, but systematic individual variability in the quadratic term was trivial. Careful attention to both population growth curve coefficients and individual growth curve variances and covariances is necessary to identify the appropriate longitudinal model.

Another measurement assumption that must be met with longitudinal data analyses is that all repeated assessments must measure the same attribute in the same metric over time. An example of an attribute that meets this assumption is vocabulary acquisition (Huttenlocher, Vasilyeva, Cymerman, & Levine, 2002), and an example of an attribute that might violate it is cognition during infancy. Cognitive tests of young infants involve a major psycho-motor component whereas tests of older individuals involve a major verbal component (Neisser, Boodoo, Bouchard, Boykin, Brody, Ceci, Halpern, Loehlink, Perloff, Steinberg, & Urbina, 1996). Furthermore, the scores from these assessments need to be in the same metric over time. Literally, it is assumed that a one-point change in the score means the same thing across the entire scale and over age. All growth curve methods rely on computing differences in scores over time, and those differences are meaningful to the extent that the metric of the assessment is consistent. Therefore, the scale needs to be consistent, which raises concerns about using raw scores. For this reason, we believe developmental age scores, Rasch scores (see Chapter II for details), or even standard scores can be very useful for describing inter-individual differences in developmental patterns.

Some, but not all, growth curve methods require that all individuals be measured at the same time points or age. Many studies attempt to measure all participants at specified intervals, creating panel data. All growth curve methods can be used with such time-structured data. Time-structured data are repeated measures data in which individuals are measured at specific time points or ages, and thus time or age can be treated as a categorical variable. Panel data are an example of time-structured data. In contrast, time can be viewed as treating time or age as a time-varying variable in data in which age at assessment is allowed to vary, either deliberately or because some data were collected late. A few methods can use the actual age or time at which data were collected as a time-varying predictor, and the accelerated longitudinal design is example of that kinds of model that deliberately plans for missing data (Graham et al., 2001).

Finally, some longitudinal methods allow the inclusion of individuals with missing data when the assumption that data are ignorably missing is met (see the chapter by Widaman for a comprehensive discussion of issues related to analyzing data with missing data). Missing data almost always occurs in longitudinal research. Data are ignorably missing when the reason the data are missing is related to the predictors and is not related to the outcome variable of interest (Schafer & Graham, 2002). For example, missing data due to attrition are probably ignorably missing, but data missing due to failure to achieve a basal score on the test are not ignorably missing. Some of the growth curve methods described below allow for the inclusion of individuals with some missing data. How the statistical method handles missing data becomes irrelevant if missing data imputation methods such as multiple imputation are used (see chapter by Widaman for details).

GROWTH CURVE METHODS

A wide variety of growth curve methods can be easily implemented with commercial software, but selection of the most appropriate methods depends on many factors. The various approaches differ in whether they allow for individual differences in intercept or rates of change (e.g., slope) and, correspondingly, whether they require a priori specification of the shape of the longitudinal trajectories. They also differ in whether they allow for ignorably missing data and for repeated measures of predictors (also called time-varying predictors) along with repeated measures of the developmental outcome. In the following pages, we briefly discuss some of the most widely used approaches, including univariate and multivariate repeated measures analysis of variance, HLM, LGC, and prototypic or mixture growth models. Table 1 provides a summary of each method's attributes and lists the currently available software that can be used to implement the method.

TABLE 1

CHARACTERISTICS OF SELECTED GROWTH CURVE METHODS

	Type of Growth Curve Method				
	Univariate	Profile	HLM	LGC	Prototypic
Models Allow For:					
Individual differences					
Intercept	Yes	Yes	Yes	Yes	No
Slope	No	Yes	Yes	Yes	No
Specifying within-subjects model	Yes	Yes	Yes	Yes	Yes
Time-varying covariates	Yes	No	Yes	Yes	No
Ignorably missing data	Yes	No	Yes	Some	Some
Assessment times that vary	Yes	No	Yes	Some	No
Measurement error in predictors	No	No	No	Yes	No
Test statistics are "valid" for moderate to large samples	No	Yes	Yes	Yes	NA
Useful Software:					
SAS (procedure)	GLM	GLM	Mixed	CALIS	Cluster
SPSS (procedure)	GLM	GLM	HLM	AMOS	Cluster
HLM			Yes		
MPlus			Yes	Yes	Yes
AMOS				Yes	
Trajectory					SAS Macro

To illustrate the various growth curve methods, the simulated data and data from a published longitudinal study were analyzed. The simulated data represents developmental data from six children who were to be measured every six months between 24 and 60 months. Because most longitudinal studies are unable to assess all children at all occasions, we have allowed for missing data (i.e., ignorably missing). Figure 1a plots the data for these six children. Most children have some missing data and they vary in level and rate of change over time. The other example data set is from the Abecedarian and CARE Projects, conducted at the Frank Porter Graham Child Development Institute (Burchinal et al., 1997). At birth, 161 low-income children were randomly assigned to a child care intervention or control group. Table 2 contains descriptive statistics of the sample and Figure 2a shows plots of scores for randomly selected individuals.

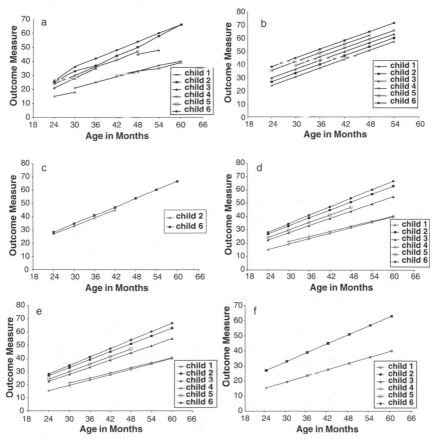

FIGURE 1.—Estimated growth curves from example data: (a) longitudinal data; (b) "univariate" growth curves; (c) profile analysis growth curves; (d) hierarchical linear models (HLM) growth curves; (e) latent growth curves (LGC); and (f) prototypic growth curves

73

TABLE 2

CHILD CARE INTERVENTION STUDY DATA

	Age (in years)						
	2	3	4	5	6.5	8	12
N	163	160	159	155	150	174	174
Home							
M	.61	.66	.71	.74	.74	.69	.69
SD	.12	.13	.12	.11	.11	.09	.09

Child IQ by child care treatment

	Stanford Binet				WPPSIWISC-R		
	2	3	4	5	6.5	8	12
Treatment							
M	97.1	101.8	101.1	102.4	99.8	98.4	95.8
SD	11.3	12.9	10.8	10.5	12.9	12.0	10.2
Control							
M	85.7	87.5	90.8	94.6	93.6	92.2	90.6
SD	11.5	14.2	12.4	14.0	13.0	12.4	11.5

Note.—40% of sample received the child care treatment. HOME was not administered at 6.5 or 12 years, so previous score was carried forward.

Children's intelligence was tested annually between two and five years of age and then every 18 months after entry to school. About one-third of the children missed at least one assessment, but none of the missing data was due to factors associated with the child's intelligence (e.g., can be considered ignorably missing). In most cases, it was due to the family's temporary relocation from the area. We also measured aspects of the child's life that were changing (i.e., quality of home environment as measured by the Home Observation for Measuring the Environment [HOME; Caldwell & Bradley, 1984]) and aspects we presumed to be unchanging (e.g., maternal IQ). This example was used to demonstrate how the various methods deal with missing data, time-varying covariates, and appropriately adjust for correlations in the repeated assessments.

Univariate Repeated Measures Approach

The original repeated measures analysis method is called the univariate repeated measures analysis of variance or mixed models. It was widely used by developmentalists until about 1980 and continues to be used by other psychologists from other disciplines. This method assumes there are

74

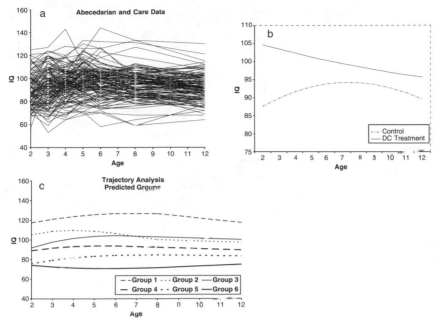

FIGURE 2.—Child care intervention study data and estimated group growth curves: (a) longitudinal data; (b) treatment hierarchical linear models (HLM) group curves; and (c) prototypic curves

individual differences in the level or intercept of repeated measures, but not in rates of change over time. As a consequence, this method underestimates variability and overestimates test statistics when individuals have different slopes. This limitation has been widely recognized and various approaches have been developed to provide more appropriate test statistics (see Tabachnick & Fidell, 2007, for a discussion). These approaches require deleting the data from any individual who was not observed at all time points, estimating the degree of correlation among the repeated assessments, and adjusting the degrees of freedom for error accordingly.

Growth curves for the example data sets were estimated using this approach. First, the simulated data were fit to the model without the adjustment and results are shown in Figure 1b. The growth curves are constrained to have the same slope but allowed to have different intercepts. Thus, the individual growth curves with the simulated data are poorly estimated because the marked differences in slopes are ignored. Second, the child care intervention study was analyzed with univariate growth curve methods, using the corrections for type-I error inflation (Tabachnick & Fidell, 2007). This deletes all data for individuals who have any missing data on variables used as independent or dependent variables. Despite the fact that data were collected on 162 children, only the 139 subjects with

TABLE 3

GROWTH CURVE PARAMETER ESTIMATES: CHILD CARE INTERVENTION STUDY

	Type of Growth Model			
	Univariate	Multivariate	HLM	LGC
	139	139	162	162
N	F	F	F	t^2
Child care treatment	29.6***	29.6***	30.8***	34.7***
Maternal IQ	10.5***	10.5***	34.5***	9.7***
Home environment	24.2***	24.2***	4.7***	7.7***
Age × child care treatment	7.7***			
Linear		14.3***	35.1***	13.9***
Quadratic		18.9***	18.4***	4.0*
Age × maternal IQ	2.2			
Linear		4.8*	.8	6.3*
Quadratic		1.7	1.2	2.7
Age × home environment	1.8			
Linear		2.0	9.2**	.5
Quadratic		6.1*	1.4	.4

Note.— *$p < .05$, **$p < .01$, ***$p < .001$.

complete data could be included in the analysis. Time-varying predictors are not allowed, so we computed the mean HOME score from our repeated assessments, thereby creating a time-invariant predictor. The analysis included the child care treatment, maternal IQ, the mean of the repeated HOME scores, age at assessment as a categorical variable (i.e., the six dummy variables representing age contrasted each of the first six assessment ages with the final assessment age) and interactions between the other variables and age. The analysis ignored all individual differences in rates of change over time and poorly estimated the main effects for age and interactions involving age. The test statistics are shown in the first column of Table 3. As you can see, this analysis indicated that the child care treatment, $F(1, 135) = 29.6$, $p < .001$, maternal IQ, $F(1, 135) = 10.5$, $p < .001$, and HOME, $F(1, 135) = 24.2$, $p < .001$, were related to the level of the children's IQ, but only the child care treatment was related to patterns of change over time, $F(6, 135) = 7.7$, $p < .001$. The analysis treated time as a categorical variable, so the tests for age were across all ages and did not allow us to distinguish among linear, quadratic, or higher order patterns of change.

Multivariate Repeated Measures Analysis

Once computers became faster and more accessible about 30 years ago, we were able to switch from these univariate growth curve methods to the multivariate repeated measures approach, or profile analysis (Tabachnick & Fidell, 2007). The multivariate approach was a marked improvement over the univariate growth curve methods because individual differences in slopes were allowed. That is, separate growth curves are estimated for each individual, and those individual growth curve parameters are used to estimate group growth curves. The individual growth curve parameters are estimated using ordinary least squares, and the group growth curve parameters are estimated as unweighted or simple means of the corresponding individual growth curve parameters. For example, the intercept for a given group is estimated as the mean of the individual intercepts for all individuals in that group. This flexibility in modeling produces valid test statistics when sample sizes are moderate to large and appropriate polynomial models are selected to describe individual growth curves. However, the multivariate approach also has major limitations. Like the univariate approach, this method also excludes individuals with any missing data and cannot easily incorporate time-varying covariates (see Table 1).

Profile analyses were conducted using the simulated and intervention study data. Using the simulated data, growth curves are estimated only for the two individuals with complete data (see Figure 1c), but those two individuals were allowed to have different growth curves. Using the child care intervention study, the profile analysis included data from 139 children in the sample, excluding children with missing data. Orthogonal contrasts among the dependent variables computed linear and quadratic trends over time and allowed us to test whether the selected predictors were related to either linear or quadratic change. The F-tests from the analysis are shown in the second column of Table 3. Figure 2b shows the estimated growth curves for the treatment and control groups. As in the univariate method, the time-varying predictor, HOME scores, had to be averaged and included as a between-subjects predictor. The F-tests for child care treatment, maternal IQ, and HOME are constrained to be identical under the univariate and multivariate approaches (see columns 2 and 3 in Table 3). This is because the main effects with both models test for differences related to those factors in the individual growth curve intercept estimated as the mean of the repeated assessments for that individual. In contrast, the two approaches describe patterns of change quite differently because the profile analysis allows for individual differences in individual growth curve linear and quadratic slopes, using a multivariate test to ask if both linear and quadratic change is related to the predictors. The two child care groups differed in their linear, $F(1, 135) = 14.3$, $p < .001$, and quadratic, $F(1, 135) = 18.9$, $p < .001$, rates of change over time. Further, higher maternal IQ was associated with more linear gains over time, $F(1, 135) = 4.8$, $p < .05$, and higher averaged-over-time HOME scores were associated with more curvature, $F(1, 135) = 6.1$, $p < .05$.

Hierarchical Linear Models (HLM)

As computers became even faster and more accessible in the 1980s, methods that addressed many of these limitations of the univariate and multivariate approaches became feasible. General linear mixed models, called HLM by social scientists, were developed to describe intra-individual developmental patterns and identify inter-individual predictors of developmental patterns (Laird & Ware, 1982; Bryk & Raudenbush, 1992; Raudenbush & Bryk, 2002; Singer & Willett, 2003). Like the multivariate growth curve approach, HLM estimates an individual growth curve for each individual and a group growth curve from the individual growth curve parameters. Unlike the multivariate growth curve approach, the individual growth curves are estimated using empirical Bayesian or maximum likelihood methods and are weighted to include information from both the individual's and the entire sample's data. Individual growth curves are smoothed toward the group growth curve if they appear too different under the assumption that error accounts for the reason that the individual curve seems deviant. That is, group growth curve parameters are estimated as the weighted mean of the corresponding individual curve parameters from individuals in that group. Larger weights are given to individuals with more repeated assessments and smaller weights to the individuals whose data appear deviant compared with the rest of their group. This smoothing of individual curves and weighting of group curve parameters has been referred to as borrowing strength and can greatly increase the precision of parameter estimates and power to identify predictors of developmental patterns (Raudenbush & Bryk, 2002; Singer & Willett, 2003).

The advantages to using this approach can be seen in Table 1 and Figure 1d. Individual growth curves are allowed to vary in terms of both intercepts and slopes. This approach can be used when data are ignorably missing, eliminating the need to delete individuals with missing data. It can easily include time-varying covariates and assessment times that vary across individuals. The methods are asymptotic, but test statistics should be valid when sample sizes are moderate to large and distributional assumptions are met. The necessary sample size will depend on the number of individuals in the sample, the number of repeated assessments, the distribution of the variables, and the number of parameters estimated in the model. As a very rough guideline, group sizes of 30–50 should provide reasonable test statistics when variables are normally distributed and five or fewer variables are included to predict intercepts and slopes.

HLM analyses of the two example data sets demonstrate these characteristics. Figure 1d shows that we were able to estimate individual growth curves for all six individuals and they were allowed to vary in level and rates of change over time. The HLM analysis of the child care intervention data predicted IQ trajectories with linear individual growth curves, quadratic group curves, time-varying assessments of the HOME, and a single time-invariant measure of maternal IQ. As shown in the third column of Table 3, the children who received the child care intervention tended to have higher IQ scores over time, $F(1, 464) = 30.8$, $p < .005$, to show more linear gain over time, $F(1, 464) = 35.1$, $p < .001$, and have more curvature in their trajectories, $F(1, 464) = 18.4$, $p < .001$. The treatment and control group growth curves were almost identical to those estimated using the multivariate approach shown in Figure 2b so an additional plot is not provided. In addition, results suggested that maternal IQ was directly related to children's IQ trajectories, $F(1, 464) = 34.5$, $p < .001$, but was not related to patterns of change over time when the concurrent HOME was also considered. The HOME was related to children's IQ overall, $F(1, 464) = 4.7$, $p < .05$, and to linear increases over time, $F(1, 464) = 9.2$, $p < .01$. Compared with the multivariate analysis approach, HLM indicated a different role for maternal IQ and the HOME in predicting cognitive trajectories because it related the HOME scores to the IQ scores from the same assessment time, whereas the multivariate approach included the HOME as the averaged-over-time score for each family. Finally, using a series of analyses to test mediation (MacKinnon, Lockwood, Hoffman, West, & Sheets, 2002), we were able to provide evidence supporting a mediated path from maternal IQ through HOME to cognitive development (Burchinal et al., 1997).

Latent Growth Curves (LGC)

LGC have been proposed and can be estimated with widely used software. This approach has been shown to be equivalent to HLM in approach and estimation of individual growth curves (Curran, 2003). Muthén and his colleagues (Muthén & Curran, 1997; Muthén & Muthén, 2000; Muthén, 2004) popularized a structural equation modeling (SEM) approach in which fixed paths in the measurement model estimate individual growth curves and estimated paths in the SEM describe direct and indirect associations among the latent variables. The model assumes that all individuals were measured at each time point, and estimates a latent intercept and slope for each individual by fixing the loadings of the observed variables on these latent variables. The most recent version of the SEM software MPlus allows for both ignorably missing data for time-structured data and for data in which assessment times are allowed to vary among individuals (Muthén, 2004). The loading of all repeated assessments is constrained to "1" to specify the latent intercept, and the latent linear slope loadings are constrained to the time of assessment. Nonlinear slopes can be specified, and alternative time metrics such as orthogonal polynomials can be used.

The LGC approach has numerous strengths (see Table 1). It allows for time-varying covariates by specifying latent intercepts and slopes in the measurement model for each time-varying covariate, and allowing the latent intercepts and slopes to be related across multiple time-varying variables. Essentially, both level and change in one variable can be used to predict level and change in other variables. Error in assessment is considered in the measurement model, and errors can be allowed to correlate.

This approach offers major advantages and a few disadvantages over other methods. The major advantages of this approach compared with all other approaches include its ability to account for some error in predictors and to test mediation hypotheses. The major disadvantage of this approach in easy-to-implement software packages includes its reliance on time-structured data and a slight reduction in power compared with HLM due to the fact that the HLM approach smoothes the estimates parameters of the individual growth curves.

LGCs are presented using the simulated data and the child care intervention data. To compare the LGC and HLM approaches, we made two decisions in fitting the models. First, Figures 1d and e show that the estimated individual growth curves from the LGC and HLM approaches are identical. This occurred because we intentionally fixed the loadings in the LGC approach to equal those under the HLM approach. Second, we fitted a reduced model to the child care intervention data rather than the more complicated model that included several time-varying covariates that has been previously published using HLM (Burchinal et al., 1997). It was necessary to reduce the number of estimated parameters under the LGC approach because of the small sample size.

Results from the LGC are shown in the final column of Table 3. Individual quadratic growth curves were estimated by fixing paths to the repeated IQ assessments, using a value of "1" as the designated path for the intercept, age in years at assessment minus five (i.e., age at the end of treatment) as the designated path for the linear slope, and that age squared as the designated path for the quadratic slope. LGC were estimated for IQ and HOME scores. The treatment and control group growth curves were almost identical to those estimated using the multivariate and HLM approach shown in Figure 2b, so an additional plot is not provided. Overall, the results are quite similar to the multivariate and HLM analysis results, suggesting that child care treatment, maternal IQ, and the quality of the home environment were related to the overall level of intellectual development, and that the child care treatment and maternal IQ were related to patterns of change. Findings regarding the main effect of the HOME on IQ are more similar for the multivariate and LGC analyses than for the HLM analysis. This is because both the multivariate and LGC analyses included the time-varying predictor, HOME, averaged over time for family. The LGC measurement model for the home estimates the HOME intercept as the mean of the repeated HOME scores for a given individual, producing the same under the model that we created when used the mean HOME scores in the multivariate analyses. In contrast, the HLM analysis linked each HOME score to the IQ score from that assessment point. Additionally, the LGC extends the findings from the multivariate and HLM analyses by testing the association between linear change over time on the HOME and IQ development. Furthermore, unlike the HLM analysis, we were able to test the mediation of maternal IQ through HOME (i.e., an indirect path) within the LGC model and did not have to use additional models to derive the indirect path as was necessary for HLM.

Prototypic or Mixture Growth Curves

The prototypic growth curve methods are person-oriented analyses of longitudinal data. They are based on the assumption that there are a small number of qualitatively different LGC that underlie development within the populations sampled (Nagin, 1999; Muthén, 2001). It is assumed that the LGC differ markedly from each other and account for much of the individual differences observed in patterns of change over time.

At least three approaches have been used to estimate prototypic growth curves. The p-type factor analysis was used in the 1960s and 1970s (e.g., the seminal monograph on cognitive development by McCall, Appelbaum, & Hogarty, 1973), but has not been used recently. This type of factor analysis involves factor analysis of the correlation matrix, estimating combinations of patterns of change on a single variable across people instead of factors across variables. Cluster analysis of longitudinal data seeks to identify homogeneous subgroups of people who show similar patterns of change over time on a single variable within groups and qualitatively different patterns across groups.

Semiparametric mixture models (also known as trajectory analysis) as popularized by Nagin and Tremblay (1999) has become a very popular method. Trajectory analysis assumes the presence of distinct groups with differing growth trajectories within the population. A polynomial or nonlinear model is used to relate age to the outcome. The method allows for missing observations and censored measurement distributions that result in clustering at the scale's minimum or maximum. This method requires the analyst to specify the number of groups present in the population. Essential to this method are posterior probability estimates of group membership that are produced for each individual (i.e., the probability of belonging to each group). The individual is consequently assigned to the group for which they have the highest probability of membership. Once group membership has been assigned, multinomial regression can be performed to investigate the relationship between covariates and the group growth trajectories. Each individual's probability of membership in their assigned group is used as the regression weight in the multinomial analysis.

A similar approach, developed by Muthén and Muthén (2000), is also quite popular. Their approach classifies each individual into one prototypic group and allows for individual variability within the prototypic group. Because the prototypic groups are defined within a measurement model, this approach also allows for modeling differences among prototypic groups within a SEM.

Analyses of the two example data sets using Nagin's semiparametric mixture growth approach (Nagin, 1999) are presented. Analysis of the simulated data, shown in Figure 1f, reveals that two prototypic patterns describe the trajectories of all six children and values were assigned to each child that represented the extent their individual growth curves were similar to the each of the two prototypic curves. The trajectory analysis of the intervention study data included six latent growth trajectories based on the Bayesian Information Criterion. The analysis procedure estimated these six trajectories and assigned six probability values to each child representing the likelihood that the child's individual growth curve resembled each LGC. Each child was assigned to the latent curve with the largest probability value. Figure 2c presents the estimated and actual mean growth trajectories for each group. Group 1 represents a small group of children ($n = 5$) with high IQ scores at age 2 who continued to have high test scores throughout the observation period. Children in Group 2 are children who tested above average early but consequently regressed toward an average score by age 8. Groups 3 and 4 consist of children with similar below average test scores (approximately 90) at age 2 but later diverge such that group 3 shows increasing test scores which eventually achieve average scores. A similar pattern was observed for groups 5 and 6. The initial test scores are considerable lower (approximately 75), but group 5 test scores increase, while group 6 test scores remain nearly constant.

Of special interest for this analysis was identifying factors that discriminate between children showing different patterns of change over time (i.e., groups 3 and 5 vs. groups 4 and 6, respectively). To investigate these factors, we performed a multinomial analysis predicting group membership from child care intervention, mother's IQ, and the averaged-over-time HOME scores. Child care treatment, mother's IQ, and the HOME score were all significantly predictive of membership in group 3 (below average-to-increasing) compared with group 4 (below normal-to-maintaining). Children who received the child care treatment were four times more likely to be in group 3 than group 4.

Comparison of Methods

The degree to which the mixture models (i.e., person-centered approaches) are distinct from HLM or LGC (i.e., variable-centered approaches) has been debated. It is clear that all growth models are sensitive to distributional violations, but the mixture growth approaches are particularly vulnerable (Bauer & Curran, 2003). Some argue that all growth modeling methods should be labeled person-centered because the analysis is based on the repeated assessments of the individual (Molenaar, 2004), while others argue that the growth mixture models are convenient representations of complex individual trajectories (Eggleston, Laub, & Sampson, 2004). To some degree, such debate can be practically resolved if attention is paid to selecting the method most closely aligned with the theoretical model of change (Collins, 2006) and that provides the most parsimonious and clear interpretation of the findings (Cudeck & Henly, 2003).

The five growth curve methods differ in many ways but tend to yield similar conclusions when used to analyze these two data sets. The univariate and prototypic/person-oriented approaches provide the poorest estimation of individual growth curves but provide interesting groups showing different developmental patterns. Accordingly, the HLM and LGC approaches provide the best estimation of individual growth curves and will have the most power to identify predictors of individual developmental patterns unless there are unspecified subgroups in the sample that show very different patterns of change over time.

The univariate approach is clearly the least desirable method for estimating individual growth curves. Theoretically, it does not allow for individual differences in rates of change over time and, accordingly, will result in poorly specified growth curve models and associated test statistics. There seems to be no real advantage to using this approach in today's world of fast computers. The multivariate approach improves upon the univariate approach but still is more restrictive than either the HLM or LGC approaches. The inability to easily accommodate time-varying predictors or individuals with some ignorably missing data makes this approach less desirable.

The mixture growth model identified latent profiles, not individual developmental trajectories. As such, it answers a different question. It does not allow for individual differences in developmental patterns among children who are classified as showing the same LGC. Furthermore, the ability to identify predictors of developmental patterns was compromised by the classification of individual longitudinal data into categorical data in our example. It is not surprising that we had less power to identify predictors of intellectual developmental patterns when the outcome measure is a categorical variable than when the outcome variables are individual growth curve intercepts and slopes.

The HLM and LGC approaches provide the most flexible and precise estimates of individual developmental patterns and identification of predictors of developmental patterns. There are minor differences in how the HLM and LGC approaches estimate individual growth curves using the defaults in commonly used software, but larger differences in how they relate the predictors to patterns of development. Both the HLM and LGC estimate a separate intercept and slope for each child. The LGC approach estimates individual developmental patterns for each longitudinal outcome and predictor and relates levels and rates of change in the outcome and the predictors; whereas the HLM approach links level and rate of change in the outcome variable to co-occurring changes in the predictors.

The HLM and LGC approaches also differ in terms of their power to detect mediators and moderators (Singer & Willett, 2003). Currently, only the HLM approach can be used with easy-to-use software when data are not time structured. The HLM approach is ideal for identifying moderators. It is easy to create interaction terms by crossing either categorical variables representing groups of interest or continuous variables. There is more power to detect interactions involving rates of change when default options are used with the HLM approach in most circumstances because the HLM approach smoothes by estimating individual growth curve parameters from both the group's and individual's data whereas the LCG approach estimates those parameters only from the individual's data. In contrast, the LGC approach provides considerably power to detect mediators. Only the LGC approach provides to estimate the indirect path suggesting mediation within a single analysis model.

Despite the many differences of the selected methods, it is reassuring that similar conclusions were reached when all five approaches were used to analyze the data from a child care intervention study. In all analyses, higher IQ scores were linked to the child care treatment and were related to both maternal IQ and the family environment. The models that allowed for individuals to show different rates of change over time actually provided better identification of predictors of development. The HLM approach clearly suggested that children in the child care treatment group showed less change over time in IQ, whereas the LGC approach provided clearer evidence suggesting that quality of the family environment mediated the association between maternal and child IQ.

In conclusion, growth curve analyses provide developmentalists with powerful statistical methods for describing individual patterns of development and for identifying predictors of individual developmental patterns. Careful selection of the type of method involves considering characteristics of the data and the model. One must consider whether the attribute is measured with sufficient precision to estimate actual developmental functions or approximate developmental patterns, and whether the measurement resulted in ignorably missing data, time-structured data, time-varying covariates, and error in predictors and outcomes. It is important to carefully select both the model that describes individual developmental patterns and the model that identifies predictors of development. Model selection must also take into account whether the primary questions involve mediators or moderators. Consideration of each of these factors can result in the selection of the growth curve methodology that should provide the most complete description of individual patterns of development and the most powerful approach to identifying predictors of development. The optimal statistical approach represents the theoretical model of change by describing the developmental patterns dictated by that model using the data collected by the developmental project.

ACKNOWLEDGMENT

We would like to thank Frances Campbell for allowing us to use examples from the Abecedarian Project and its follow-up project, Project CARE, and the many investigators for whom we have provided data analysis over the past 25 years.

REFERENCES

Bauer, D. J., & Curran, P. J. (2003). Distributional assumptions of growth mixture models: Implication for overextraction of latent trajectory classes. *Psychological Methods*, **8**, 338–363.

Blanton, H., & Jaccard, J. (2006). Arbitrary metrics in psychology. *American Psychologist*, **61**, 27–41.

Bock, R. D., Wainer, H., Peterson, A., Thissen, D., Jurray, J., & Roch, A. (1973). A parameterization for individual human growth curves. *Human Biology*, **45**, 63–80.

Bryk, A. S., & Raudenbush, S. W. (1992). *Hierarchical linear models*. Newberry Park, CA: Sage Publications.

Burchinal, M. R., & Appelbaum, M. I. (1991). Estimating individual developmental functions: Various methods and their assumptions. *Child Development*, **62**, 23–43.

Burchinal, M. R., Campbell, F. A., Bryant, D. B., Wasik, B. H., & Ramey, C. T. (1997). Early intervention and mediating processes in cognitive performance of children of low-income African-American families. *Child Development*, **68**, 935–954.

Caldwell, B., & Bradley, R. (1984). *HOME observation for measurement of the environment*. Little Rock, AK: University of Arkansas at Little Rock.

Clogg, C. C. (1995). Latent class models. In G. Arminger, C. C. Clogg & M. E. Sobel (Eds.), *Handbook of statistical modeling for the social and behavioral sciences* (pp. 311–359). New York: Plenum.

Collins, L. M. (2006). Analysis of longitudinal data: The integration of theoretical model, temporal design, and statistical model. *Annual Review of Psychology*, **57**, 505–528.

Cudeck, R., & Henly, S. J. (2003). A realistic perspective on pattern representation in growth data: Comment on Bauer and Curran. *Psychological Methods*, **8**, 378–383.

Diggle, P., Liang, K., & Zeger, S. (1994). *Analysis of longitudinal data*. Oxford: Clarendon Press.

Eggleston, E. P., Laub, J. H., & Sampson, R. J. (2004). Methodological sensitivities to latent class analysis of long-term criminal trajectories. *Journal of Quantitative Criminology*, **20**, 1–26.

Gebotys, R (1993). *How the number of response categories influence the ANOVA and Pearson R*. Paper presented at the annual meeting of the American Statistical Association, San Francisco, CA.

Graham, J. W., Taylor, B. J., & Cumsville, P. E. (2001). Planned missing-data designs in the analysis of change. In L. Collins & A. Sayer (Eds.), *New methods for the analysis of change* (pp. 333–353). Washington, DC: American Psychological Association.

Huttenlocher, J., Vasilyeva, M., Cymerman, E., & Levine, S. (2002). Language input and child syntax. *Cognitive Psychology*, **45**, 337–374.

Laird, N. M., & Ware, J. H. (1982). Random-effects models for longitudinal data. *Biometrics*, **38**, 963–974.

MacKinnon, D. P., Lockwood, C. M., Hoffman, J. M., West, S. G., & Sheets, V. (2002). A comparison of methods to test mediation and other intervening variable effects. *Psychological Methods*, **7** (1), 83–104.

McArdle, J. J., & Nesselroade, J. R. (2003). Growth curve analysis in contemporary psychological research. In W. Velicer & J. Schinka (Eds.), *Handbook of psychology: Research methods in psychology* (pp. 447–480). New York: Wiley.

McCall, R. B., Appelbaum, M. I., & Hogarty, P. S. (1973). Developmental changes in mental performance. *Monographs of the Society for Research in Child Development*, **38** (3, Ser150).

Molenaar, P. C. M. (2004). A manifesto on psychology as idiographic science: Bringing the person back into scientific psychology, this time forever. *Measurement Interdisciplinary Research Perceptive*, **2**, 201–218.

Muthén, B. (2001). Second-generation structural equation modeling with a combination of categorical and continuous latent variables: New opportunities for latent class-latent profile growth modeling. In L. Collins & A. Sayer (Eds.), *New methods for the analysis of change* (pp. 289–322). Washington, DC: American Psychological Association.

Muthén, B. (2004). Latent variable analysis: Growth mixture modeling and related techniques for longitudinal data. In D. Kaplan (Ed.), *Handbook of quantitative methodology for the social sciences* (345–368). Newbury Park, CA: Sage.

Muthén, B. O., & Curran, P. J. (1997). General longitudinal modeling of individual differences in experimental designs: A latent variable framework for analysis and power estimation. *Psychological Methods*, **2**, 371–402.

Muthén, B., & Muthén, L. (2000). Integrating person-centered and variable-centered analysis: Growth mixture modeling with latent trajectory classes. *Alcoholism: Clinical and Experimental Research*, **24**, 882–891.

Nagin, D. (1999). Analyzing developmental trajectories: A semiparametric, group-based approach. *Psychological Methods*, **4**, 139–157.

Nagin, D., & Tremblay, R. E. (1999). Trajectories of physical aggression, opposition, and hyperactivity on the path to physically violent and nonviolent juvenile delinquency. *Child Development*, **70**, 1181–1196.

Neisser, U., Boodoo, G., Bouchard, T. J., Boykin, A. W., Brody, N., Ceci, S. J., Halpern, D. F., Loehlink, J. C., Perloff, R., Steinberg, R., & Urbina, S. (1996). Intelligence: Knowns and unknowns. *American Psychologist*, **51**, 77–101.

Raudenbush, S. W., & Bryk, A. S. (2002). *Hierarchical linear models: Applications and data analysis methods* (2nd ed.). Newbury Park, CA: Sage.

Rogosa, D. R., Brandt, D., & Willett, J. (1982). A growth curve approach to the measurement of change. *Psychological Bulletin*, **90**, 726–748.

Schafer, J. L., & Graham, J. W. (2002). Missing data: Our view of the state of the art. *Psychological Methods*, **7** (2), 147–177.

Singer, J. D., & Willett, J. B. (2003). *Applied longitudinal data analysis: Modeling change and event occurrence*. New York, NY: Oxford Press.

Tabachnick, B. G., & Fidell, L. S. (2007). *Using multivariate statistics* (5th ed.). Boston, MA: Pearson Educational Inc.

Vonesh, E. F. (1996). *Linear and nonlinear models for the analysis of repeated measurements*. New York, NY: Marcel Dekker.

Willett, J. B., Singer, J., & Martin, N. (1997). The design and analysis of longitudinal studies of development and psychopathology in context: Statistical models and methodological recommendations. *Development and Psychopathology*, **10**, 395–426.

V. CONTEMPORARY ADVANCES AND CLASSIC ADVICE FOR ANALYZING MEDIATING AND MODERATING VARIABLES

Analysis of mediating and moderating variables is often fundamental to the study of human development. Few developmental researchers, however, take advantage of contemporary advances for the analysis of mediating variables and classic advice for the analysis of moderating variables, both of which have lately become more user-friendly—for example, through web-based tools. In this chapter, we review statistical techniques for the study of mediating and moderating variables with three goals in mind: (1) communicating the current consensus on best statistical practices, (2) providing a primer for those unfamiliar with these practices, and (3) directing readers toward resources that simplify their application.

DEFINING THE TERMS

A mediator is an intervening variable that accounts, at least in part, for the relation between a predictor and an outcome variable (Baron & Kenny, 1986). That is, the predictor influences the outcome indirectly, by influencing a mediating variable which then influences the outcome. In developmental research, variables that are more distal to developmental functioning exert their influence via mediating variables that are more proximal. By analyzing mediating variables, developmental researchers seek to understand the mechanisms that directly influence development, and the chains of events through which those mechanisms exert their influence.

A moderator is a variable that qualifies the association between a predictor and outcome variable (e.g., Aiken & West, 1991; Baron & Kenny, 1986; Cohen & Cohen, 1983). Put another way, the effect of the predictor on the outcome shifts, depending on values of the moderator variable. In developmental research, the additive effects of variables do not always provide adequate explanations, because variables influencing development often do so by modifying other variables' effects (e.g., Gottlieb, 2003; Magnusson & Stattin, 1998; Parke & Buriel, 1998). By analyzing moderating variables, developmental researchers consider the ways in which some processes amplify, diminish, or qualitatively alter the influences of others.

BEST STATISTICAL PRACTICES FOR TESTING MEDIATION HYPOTHESES

Mediating processes, also called indirect effects, can be examined through both experimental and nonexperimental research; in the nonexperimental case, our focus is on understanding indirect relations between predictors and outcomes. As an example of mediation in nonexperimental research, consider work by Farver, Xu, Eppe, Fernandez, and Schwartz (2005) who studied whether the association between mothers' exposure to violence in the community and distress among their preschool-age children might be mediated by a third variable, mothers' depression. The authors report that maternal exposure to violence predicts higher levels of child distress. The authors also found, however, that this relation exists, at least in part, due to an indirect path from maternal violence exposure to heightened depressive symptomatology, which, in turn, leads to heightened child distress.

A Popular, but Problematic Approach to Examining Mediation

The causal steps approach for identifying mediation processes (Judd & Kenny, 1981a, b; Baron & Kenny, 1986) requires that researchers estimate regression coefficients for the effects of predictor on mediator (i.e., α in Figure 1), predictor on outcome (i.e., τ in Figure 1), and mediator on outcome controlling for the predictor (i.e., β in Figure 1). Although the causal steps approach has been popular among researchers, most have overlooked Baron and Kenny's (1986) recommendation for testing the significance of the mediated effect (i.e., $\alpha\beta$) using the method developed by Sobel (1982).

Relying solely on the causal steps approach to identify mediation is limiting in at least three regards (MacKinnon, Lockwood, Hoffman, West, & Sheets, 2002; Preacher & Hayes, 2004, 2006). First, the causal steps approach does not provide a direct hypothesis test for mediation. Second, it is not easily adaptable to situations where there exist two or more mediating pathways between predictor and outcome. Third, the causal steps method lacks statistical power.

Evidence for the lack of power comes from work by MacKinnon et al. (2002), who compared several methods and concluded that Type-II errors occur more frequently with the causal steps approach than they do with alternatives. This high Type-II error rate reflects the requirement that the predictor be significantly related to the outcome before controlling for the

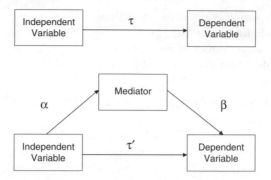

FIGURE 1.—Direct and mediated pathways linking a predictor and outcome variable. Pathway τ depicts the association between the predictor and outcome variable before controlling for the potential mediator. Pathway τ' depicts the direct association between the predictor and outcome variable, once controlling for the indirect association between the predictor and outcome variable via the mediator (i.e., $\alpha\beta$).

mediator (i.e., that τ in Figure 1 be nonzero). As Shrout and Bolger (2002) note, this requirement is unrealistic for developmental processes, where distal influences can have subtle effects across time if more proximal mediators are not considered.

The literature contains examples where a predictor significantly affects a mediator, and the mediator in turn significantly affects an outcome, even though the simple association between predictor and outcome is not significant itself (MacKinnon, Krull, & Lockwood, 2000). Such instances are referred to as inconsistent mediation (Davis, 1985; MacKinnon et al., 2000). Inconsistent mediation occurs when the sign of association (positive or negative) is opposite for the direct and indirect links between the predictor and outcome variables. We use the term mediation in this chapter to refer to associations between variables that are indirect via one or more intervening variables, including inconsistent mediation effects.

Recommended Mediation Analyses

In view of the limitations of the causal steps method, what approach can we recommend? With large enough samples (i.e., $n > 400$), the best approach is often a Sobel test (Bollen & Stine, 1990; MacKinnon et al., 2002; Preacher & Hayes, 2006; Shrout & Bolger, 2002; Stone & Sobel, 1990)

$$z = \frac{\alpha\beta}{\sqrt{\alpha^2 s_\alpha^2 + \beta^2 s_\beta^2}} \tag{1}$$

where α is the unstandardized coefficient from the regression of mediator on predictor, β is the unstandardized coefficient from the regression of outcome on mediator, s_α is the standard error for α, and s_β is the standard error for β. Under the null hypothesis H_0: $\alpha\beta = 0$, z follows a standard normal distribution. Thus, if $|z| > 1.96$, we might confidently reject the null hypothesis of no indirect effect ($p < .05$).

Note that the numerator in the Sobel equation is the product of coefficients corresponding to: (1) the estimated effect of predictor on mediator (α in Figure 1) and (2) the estimated effect of mediator on outcome (β in Figure 1). When estimated via ordinary least-squares (OLS) regression, this $\alpha\beta$ product is algebraically equivalent to the difference in the size of the direct effect before and after controlling for the mediator (i.e., $\alpha\beta = c - c'$, MacKinnon, Warsi, & Dwyer, 1995). In other words, the product of the coefficients comprising the mediated effect equals the change in the effect of the predictor on the outcome after controlling for the mediated effect.

For researchers estimating mediation using structural equation modeling programs, the Sobel test is a widely available option. For researchers estimating mediation using OLS regression, Preacher and Leonardelli (2006) offer a web-based Sobel test at www.quantpsy.org for the mediated effect of interest using the coefficients and standard errors corresponding to estimates of α and β, which are provided in default outputs from statistical programs such as SPSS, SAS, and STATA (for STATA, also see UCLA Academic Technology Services, 2006). Large-sample 95% confidence limits for the product of the coefficients can also be calculated from the formula

$$z = \alpha\beta \pm \left(\sqrt{\alpha^2 s_\alpha^2 + \beta^2 s_\beta^2}(1.96) \right) \tag{2}$$

Confidence limits constructed using this method and the Sobel test, more generally, assume that the sampling distribution of $\alpha\beta$ is approximately standard normal. This assumption, however, might not be justified when sample size is small to moderate (Bollen & Stine, 1990; MacKinnon et al., 2004; Preacher & Hayes, 2006; Shrout & Bolger, 2002).

When sample size is small to moderate ($n < 400$), the Sobel test lacks sufficient power, primarily because the small-sample sampling distribution of $\alpha\beta$ is often skewed. For such samples, more plausible confidence limits for $\alpha\beta$ can be estimated through bootstrapping (Bollen & Stine, 1990; MacKinnon et al., 2004; Preacher & Hayes, 2006; Shrout & Bolger, 2002). This method involves three steps:

1. Draw 1,000 or more artificial samples of size n by sampling with replacement from the original n observations.

2. Calculate $\alpha\beta$ in each bootstrap sample and save the resulting coefficients.

3. Estimate a confidence interval from percentiles of the boot-strapped distribution of $\alpha\beta$ coefficients.

We can reject the null hypothesis of no mediation if the bootstrapped confidence interval does not contain zero.

The option of bootstrapping the mediated effect is now available in some SEM programs (e.g., Mplus, version 3, Muthén & Muthén, 2004). In addition, the Stata program *sgmediation* provides an option for automatic bootstrapping of mediated effects. For researchers using OLS regression in SPSS and SAS, macros containing all of the necessary syntax for bootstrapping the mediated effect may be downloaded and used with the current versions of these programs (Preacher & Hayes, 2004; also, see Shrout & Bolger, 2002). Such programs estimate confidence limits using several methods. Straightforward bootstrapping infers confidence limits directly from percentiles (e.g., for 95% confidence limits, the upper and lower bounds would correspond to estimates of $\alpha\beta$ at the 97.5th and 2.5th percentiles of the bootstrapped distribution). Bias-corrected bootstrapping applies an adjustment in the central tendency of the $\alpha\beta$ estimate. MacKinnon et al. (2004) demonstrated that bias-corrected bootstrapping provides the most accurate confidence limits and the greatest statistical power to detect mediation in small to moderate-sized samples.

In summary, testing the product of the coefficients comprising the mediated effect is best practice for examining mediation. With large enough samples ($n > 400$), hypothesis tests and confidence limits can be calculated assuming normality, and using standard errors of the indirect effect as proposed by Sobel (1982). Given smaller samples, it is better to estimate the sampling distribution through bootstrapping. Current statistical programs make both options simple.

BEST STATISTICAL PRACTICES FOR TESTING MODERATION HYPOTHESES

Moderating processes, like mediating processes, can be examined through either experimental or nonexperimental studies, although in the latter case the emphasis is not necessarily causal. In regression analysis, moderator effects typically are estimated through the use of interaction terms, new variables defined as the product of a predictor variable and a moderator variable. This product or interaction term is then included in the regression as another predictor, alongside its component predictor and moderator variables themselves.

Analysis of moderating effects has become commonplace in developmental research and typically involves two steps: (1) testing whether the interaction term has a statistically significant (nonzero) effect on the outcome variable; and (2) graphing this effect to aid substantive interpretation. Further steps, based on classic advice that has rarely been followed, could add to our understanding of moderating processes (e.g., Aiken & West, 1991; Cohen & Cohen, 1983; Johnson & Neyman, 1936; Kerlinger & Pedhazur, 1973; for more recent work on this topic, see Cohen, Cohen, Aiken, & West, 2003; O'Connor, 1998; Preacher, Curran, & Bauer, in press). After first reviewing the regression equation with an interaction term, we discuss the value of taking two additional steps towards interpreting interactions. We then cite resources that help researchers carry out these additional steps.

Regression Equation With an Interaction Term

The regression equation with two predictors and an interaction term takes the following form (for a complete discussion of this topic, see Cohen et al., 2003; Hamilton, 1992):

$$\hat{Y}_i = b_0 + b_1 X_{i1} + b_2 X_{i2} + b_3 (X_{i1} X_{i2}) \tag{3}$$

In this equation, the coefficient b_0 is the intercept, or value of $\hat{Y}$ when both X variables equal 0 (a theoretical value that might or might not make any real-world sense). The coefficient b_1 is the change in $\hat{Y}$ given a 1-unit increase in X_1, *if* X_2 is equal to 0. That is, b_1 is the estimated slope of association between X_1 and Y, *if* $X_2 = 0$. Similarly, b_2 is the estimated slope of association between X_2 and Y, *if* $X_1 = 0$. Thus, the test statistic corresponding to b_1 (i.e., a t-test in OLS) establishes whether the association between X_1 and Y is statistically significant when $X_2 = 0$, and the test statistic corresponding to b_2 establishes whether the association between X_2 and Y is statistically significant if $X_1 = 0$. If 0 values make no substantive sense in the original metrics of X_1 or X_2, it might be worthwhile to center the variables as discussed as follows, so that their means become 0.

The coefficient b_3 represents the amount by which the effect of X_1 on Y changes, with each 1-unit increase in X_2. Or, equivalently, it represents the amount by which the effect of X_2 on Y changes, with each 1-unit increase in X_1. The usual t-test of coefficient b_3 evaluates whether the interaction between X_1 and X_2 is statistically significant—that is, for example, whether X_2 significantly moderates (changes) the relationship between X_1 and Y.

Centering Predictors

When predictor variables and/or moderator variables are quantitative and included in interactions, it is often helpful to center those predictors by subtracting the mean from each value, creating a new centered variable or deviation score such as $X_i^* = X_i - \overline{X}$. The mean of the new centered variable

X^* equals 0 (note that standardization has a similar effect, but it also changes the variables' units.). Although centering predictors has no effect on the interaction coefficient (e.g., b_3 in (3)), there are two potential benefits of using this strategy (Aiken & West, 1991; Cohen et al., 2003).

First, centering often reduces the problem of multicollinearity or too-high correlations among predictors, which can arise when we include product terms (interactions) together with their component variables among the predictors. As the degree of multicollinearity increases, regression estimates of the predictors' independent effects become increasingly unreliable, as revealed by their large standard errors, nonsignificant t-tests, and wild sample-to-sample variation (Aiken & West, 1991; Cohen et al., 2003; Hamilton, 1992). Second, centering makes interpretation easier for the main effects of our predictors. For example, if X_2 in (3) has been centered and hence has a mean of 0, then b_1 is the estimated association between X_1 and Y at the mean level of X_2.

Centering, however, is less helpful when predictor variables have a substantively interesting zero point. For example, Cohen et al. (2003) discuss the potential moderating influence of number of siblings for the association between child age and language development. In this case, centering the moderator variable (number of siblings) on its mean is undesirable because zero siblings is a meaningful, important state.

Simple Slopes

We might visualize the interaction by graphing a set of "simple" relationships between a predictor and outcome across several different values of a moderator. That is, we might graph simple slopes, also called conditional effects. From model (3), the estimated "simple" effect of X_1 on Y is $b_1 + (X_{i2})b_3$, where X_{i2} is any constant value selected for X_2 (e.g., $b_1 + 0b_3$ if $X_2 = 0$, $b_1 + 1b_3$ if $X_2 = 1$, $b_1 + 2b_3$ if $X_2 = 2$, $b_1 + 3b_3$ for $X_2 = 3$, etc.). Consider, for example, cases in which the moderator, X_2, is a dummy variable. In such cases, b_1 (i.e., $b_1 + 0b_3$) is the effect of X_1 on Y for $X_2 = 0$, and $b_1 + b_3$ (i.e., $b_1 + 1b_3$) is the effect of X_1 on Y for $X_2 = 1$. If the model contains variables other than the predictor, the moderator, and the interaction, then these are algebraically held constant (for example, set equal to their means) for purposes of graphing the simple slopes (see examples in Hamilton, 1992, 2006).

Is a simple slope significantly different from zero? We can evaluate this with a t-test. For example, for $b_1 + (X_{i2})b_3$:

$$t = \frac{b_1 + (X_{i2})b_3}{\sqrt{SE_{b_1}^2 + 2X_{i2}(\text{cov}_{b_1, b_3}) + (X_{i2}^2)SE_{b_i}^2}} \tag{4}$$

In (4), $SE_{b_1}^2$ is the variance of b_1, cov_{b_1,b_3} is the covariance of b_1 and b_3, and $SE_{b_3}^2$ is the variance of b_3. Thus, for any given value of the moderator, a simple slope for the association between the predictor and the outcome can be calculated and tested for significance. In fact, the simple slope relating Y to X_1 when $X_2 = 0$, as well as the corresponding standard error and statistical significance, is supplied with the default output of most statistical packages when a regression model is estimated because b_1 in (3) is the estimated slope for X_1 and Y if $X_2 = 0$.

For $X_2 \neq 0$ in (3), additional calculations are necessary to compute the simple slope and test its statistical significance. Researchers need not complete these calculations by hand. In STATA, for example, linear combinations of regression coefficients can be computed and tested following model estimation using a simple command (e.g., lincom $X_1+(X_{i2}X_3)$, where X_1 is the predictor of interest, X_{i2} is the chosen level of the moderator, and X_3 is the interaction term defined as the product of X_1 and X_2.). The Stata program *sslope* calculates, tests, and graphs simple slopes for two- or three-way interactions, including models with quadratic terms. Other user-friendly tools for estimating simple slopes in SPSS and SAS are available on the web.

Some online sources provide SPSS and SAS code that may be easily pasted into syntax files (e.g., O'Connor, 2006; Schubert & Jacoby, 2004). Others provide details on how to generate each of the statistics in equation (4) using programs such as SPSS and SAS, and then via an interactive tool will compute, graph, and estimate the significance of simple slopes (e.g., Preacher, Curran, & Bauer, 2006). Further, applications beyond those for two-variable interactions in regression are available, such as tools for estimating simple slopes from three-way interactions, multilevel models, and latent growth models are available at www.quantpsy.org (Preacher et al., 2006).

Regions of Significance

Estimating regions of significance for interactions identifies the range of moderator-variable values for which the predictor and outcome variables are significantly associated (Aiken & West, 1991; Kerlinger & Pedhazur, 1973; Preacher et al., in press). Regarding model (3), for example, the region of significance contains a range of X_2 values for which the association between X_1 and Y is nonzero. In some instances, we might use regions of significance to identify the range of values on the predictor variable for which the moderator is significantly associated with the outcome variable (i.e., the range of values on X_1 for which the association between X_2 and Y is statistically significant).

Regions of significance have upper and lower bounds that indicate a range of X_2 values for which X_1 has a significant effect on Y—typically applying an $\alpha = .05$ cutoff, although regions using more or less conservative p-values could be calculated instead. For some interactions, the association between predictor and outcome will be significant at values of the moderator above the upper bound or below the lower bound (indicating that values of the moderator falling between the bounds, the association between predictor and outcome is not significant). For other interactions, however, the association between the predictor and outcome variable will be significant at values of the moderator that fall between the upper and lower bounds.

Regions of significance generally are computed using the Johnson–Neyman technique (Johnson & Neyman, 1936). Although calculations are beyond the scope of this chapter, two points deserve mention. First, as Preacher and colleagues (Preacher, Curran, & Baver, in press) have noted, finding regions of significance can be conceptualized as working backwards through the computations for simple slopes (i.e., equation (4)). Whereas calculating simple slopes is a means of identifying a slope coefficient and its standard error using chosen values of the moderator, calculating regions of significance is a means of identifying the full range of values of the moderator for which the simple slopes would be statistically significant. Second, region of significances can also be depicted through confidence bands (i.e., the confidence interval for the association between the predictor and outcome across all levels of the moderator; Preacher et al., in press).

Regions of significance can be computed easily using the interactive calculation tool at www.quantpsy.org (Preacher et al., 2006). Calculation tools are available for two- and three-way interactions, estimated through OLS or multilevel modes. These tools include a user-friendly, point-and-click format with step-by-step instructions on how to generate the relevant estimates in common statistical programs (e.g., SPSS and SAS). In addition, after computing regions of significance, one can also plot confidence bands.

Empirical Example 1: Simple Slopes

A study by Jaffee, Moffitt, Caspi, and Taylor (2003) illustrates the interpretation of simple slopes. These authors examined fathers' levels of antisocial behavior as a possible moderator of the association between the amount of time that fathers were in the household and children's levels of antisocial behavior at age 5. Table 1 presents selected results from this study.

Children's antisocial behavior, father's antisocial behavior, and father's time spent in the household (i.e., the percent of time that the father lived in the household between child's birth and age 5) were all quantitative variables in this study. The authors centered father's antisocial behavior and father's time in the household on their respective means. Consequently, the coefficient on father's time in the household (-1.04) represents the effect

TABLE 1

SUMMARIZED RESULTS FROM JAFFEE ET AL. (2003)

Predictor	b	SE
Intercept	23.01	
Percent time in household	−1.04	1.82
Fathers' antisocial behavior	.37	.04
Antisocial behavior × percent time	.28	.08

that percent time in the household has on child's antisocial behavior *if father displayed an average level of antisocial behavior* (i.e., −1.04+(0).28). This coefficient was not statistically significant, leading to the conclusion that father's time in the household has no impact on child's antisocial behavior if father's antisocial behavior is just average.

As the authors expected, however, the interaction coefficient was significant—indicating that the effect of time fathers spent in the household depends on their level of antisocial behavior. To help interpret this interaction, Jaffee and colleagues calculated and graphed (Figure 2) predicted

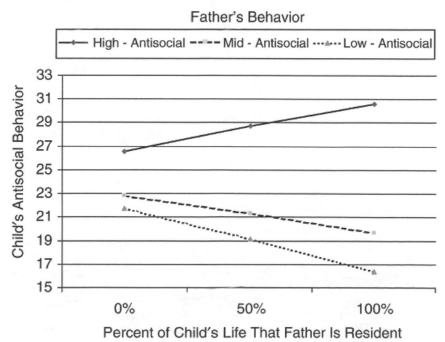

FIGURE 2.—Figure from Jaffee et al. (2003) displaying how fathers' antisocial behavior moderates the association between the percent time that fathers are in the household and children's antisocial behavior.

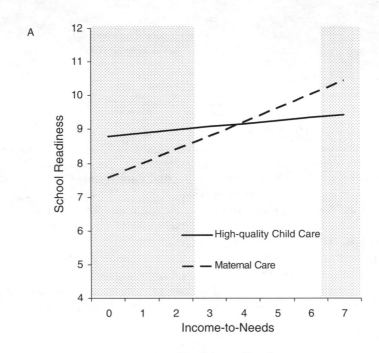

A

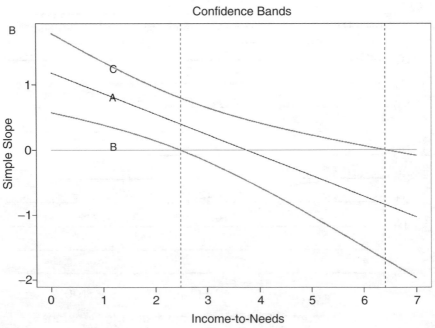

Confidence Bands

B

scores for children's antisocial behavior as a function of: (1) the amount of time fathers were in the home (i.e., 0%, 50%, and 100% of the time) and (2) fathers' levels of antisocial behavior (i.e., 15th, 50th, and 85th percentile). As is evident in Figure 2, if fathers displayed low or moderate levels of antisocial behavior, then their presence was beneficial: the more time fathers spent in the home, the lower the children's antisocial behavior. On the other hand, if the fathers displayed high levels of antisocial behavior themselves, then their presence was harmful: the more time they were home, the higher the children's antisocial behavior.

Testing the significance of the interaction term and graphing predictions about the outcome at varying levels of the predictor and moderator variables are two steps commonly completed in developmental research. Several questions remain unanswered, however, after completing these initial steps. For example, are the associations between father's time in the household and child's antisocial behavior nonzero when father's antisocial behavior is low, moderate, or high? In other words, are each of the slopes displayed in Figure 2 significant?

Jaffee and colleagues answered this question by examining simple slopes for the association between father's time in the household and child's antisocial behavior at the 15th, 50th, and 85th percentiles of father's antisocial behaviors (i.e., the slopes corresponding to the predicted scores in Figure 2). The standard errors and t-tests for these simple slopes were computed using (4). Although the simple slope for children whose fathers were at the 50th percentile was not distinguishable from 0, the slopes for children at the 15th and 85th percentiles were ($p < .05$).

At both low and high levels of paternal antisocial behavior, therefore, fathers' time in the household was *significantly* associated with child antisocial behavior—but in opposite directions. Fathers living in the household for most or all of children's lives predicted lower levels of child antisocial behavior when fathers' antisocial behavior was low, and predicted higher levels of child antisocial behavior when fathers' antisocial behavior was high.

FIGURE 3.—(a) From McCartney et al. (2003), the association between family income-to-needs and school readiness for children in maternal care and children in high-quality non-maternal care. Regions of significance are shadowed, indicating the range of income-to-needs values for which school readiness levels were significantly different for children in maternal care and children in non-maternal care. (b) Confidence bands for the McCartney et al. (2003) interaction. Line A plots variations in the slope of association between child care status and school readiness across levels of income-to-needs. Positive values on the Y-axis indicate levels of income-to-needs for which children in high-quality child care had higher levels of school readiness than children in maternal care and negative values indicate levels of income-to-needs for which children in maternal care had higher levels of school readiness than children in high-quality child care. Lines B and C are the lower and upper bounds of the 95% confidence bands, respectively. Values greater than 0 on the lower band and values less than 0 on the upper band correspond to the thresholds for the lower and upper regions of significance.

Thus, by examining these simple slopes, Jaffee and colleagues demonstrated that fathers' presence in the household is a statistically significant protective factor or risk factor in children's lives, depending on fathers' own antisocial behavior.

Empirical Example 2: Regions of Significance

To see the usefulness of examining regions of significance, consider the following example. McCartney, Dearing, and Taylor (2003) examined child care as a moderator of the association between family income-to-needs (i.e., the ratio of gross family income to family financial needs given family size) and children's school readiness at age 3. Family income-to-needs and children's school readiness are quantitative indicators; child care is a dummy variable with children in high-quality nonmaternal care coded as 1 and children in maternal care coded as 0. For analyses, the authors centered family income-to-needs on its mean.

The interaction between child care type and income-to-needs was statistically significant, indicating that the association between income-to-needs and school readiness significantly differed for children in maternal care versus children in high-quality nonmaternal care. The authors graphed both simple slopes and the region of significance for this interaction (Figure 3a). They were less interested in a region of significance for the association between income-to-needs and school readiness across levels of child care, primarily because there were only two levels of child care, and calculating simple slopes for these two groups was sufficient. Instead, the authors focused on finding levels of family income-to-needs, at which significant differences existed between the school readiness of children in maternal and high-quality nonmaternal care.

School readiness was significantly different for children in maternal and high-quality nonmaternal care either when income-to-needs was moderate to low (below its 45th percentile), or when income-to-needs was very high (above its 89th percentile). At moderate to low levels of income-to-needs, children with high-quality nonmaternal care tended to be more ready for school. At very high levels of income-to-needs, children with maternal care tended to be more ready. But among families that had moderately high levels of income-to-needs (between the 45th and 89th percentiles), school readiness was similar for both types of care.

The 95% confidence bands for the McCartney et al. example, calculated and graphed using the interactive tool at www.quantpsy.org, are displayed in Figure 3b. Line A plots variations in the size and direction of the association between child care status and school readiness across levels of income-to-needs. Positive values on the Y-axis indicate levels of income-to-needs for which children in high-quality child care had better school readiness than children in maternal care and negative values indicate the opposite, levels of income-to-needs for which children in maternal care had better school readiness than children in high-quality child care. Curves B and C mark a 95% confidence band for the simple slope of association between child-care type and school readiness.

The points at which the confidence band crosses 0 on the Y-axis correspond to the lower and upper bounds of the region of significance (indicated with vertical dashed lines). The confidence band, however, also provides information on estimate precision not available from the region of significance alone. Specifically, where the confidence band is narrow, estimates are relatively precise, and where the confidence band is wide, estimates are relatively imprecise.

INTERNET RESOURCES

User-friendly resources for applying best practices in mediation and moderation analyses are now widely available. In addition to consulting the primary sources cited in this chapter, we also recommend that researchers take advantage of the interactive tools, syntax, and programming code now available on the Internet. In light of the rapid rate that statistical programs are revised, these Internet resources are an excellent means of accessing the most up-to-date innovations. To assist in this regard, we have listed (Table 2) some popular statistical programs along with Internet sites providing tools, syntax, and code specific to these programs. Resources such as these will help make the application of state of the art mediation and moderation analyses commonplace in the study of human development.

TABLE 2

INTERNET RESOURCES FOR MEDIATION AND MODERATION SYNTAX AND PROGRAM CODE

Statistical Program	Internet Resources
HLM	www.quantpsy.org
Mplus	www.statmodel.com/ugexcerpts.shtml
	www.ats.ucla.edu/stat/
SAS	www.quantpsy.org
	www.ats.ucla.edu/stat/
	www.comm.ohio-state.edu/ahayes,
	www.public.asu.edu/~davidpm/ripl/
SPSS	www.quantpsy.org
	www.ats.ucla.edu/stat/
	www.comm.ohio-state.edu/ahayes
	www.public.asu.edu/~davidpm/ripl/
STATA	www.ats.ucla.edu/stat/

CONCLUSION

Building on classic work, methodologists have recently updated guidelines to best statistical practices for mediator and moderator analyses (e.g., Cohen et al., 2003; MacKinnon et al., 2002; O'Connor, 1998; Preacher & Hayes, 2004; Preacher et al., 2006; Shrout & Bolger, 2002). With regard to mediation, calculating and testing the product of the coefficients comprising the mediated effect is the recommended analytic strategy. When sample size is large, products of the coefficients can be tested using a Sobel test statistic. When sample size is small or moderate, bias-corrected bootstrap confidence limits provide a plausible alternative. With regard to moderation, testing the significance of the interaction term and graphing predicted scores are necessary, but not sufficient, initials steps. These should be supplemented by examining simple slopes and regions of significance.

Pathways of development are often determined by chains of events in which more distal processes influence growth through more proximal processes. In addition, factors influencing development often do so by modifying the effects of one another. Thus, mediator and moderator analyses are fundamental in answering developmental science questions. Fortunately, easy-to-use resources now exist to help researchers apply both contemporary advances and classic advice.

REFERENCES

Aiken, L. S., & West, S. G. (1991). *Multiple regression: Testing and interpreting interactions*. Newbury Park, CA: Sage Publications.

Baron, R. M., & Kenny, D. A. (1986). The moderator–mediator variable distinction in social psychological research: Conceptual, strategic, and statistical considerations. *Journal of Personality and Social Psychology*, **51**, 1173–1182.

Bollen, K. A., & Stine, R. (1990). Direct and indirect effects: Classical and bootstrap estimates of variability. *Sociological Methodology*, **20**, 115–140.

Cohen, J., & Cohen, P. (1983). *Applied multiple regression/correlation analysis for the social sciences* (2nd ed.). Hillsdale, NJ: Lawrence Erlbaum.

Cohen, J., Cohen, P., Aiken, L. S., & West, S. G. (2003). *Applied multiple regression/correlation analysis for the social sciences* (3rd ed.). Mahwah, NJ: Lawrence Erlbaum.

Davis, J. A. (1985). The logic of causal order. In J. L. Sullivan & R. G. Niemi (Series Eds.), *Quantitative applications in the social sciences: Vol. 5*. Beverly Hills, CA: Sage Publications.

Farver, J. M., Xu, Y., Eppe, S., Fernandez, A., & Schwartz, D. (2005). Community violence, family conflict, and preschoolers' socioemotional functioning. *Developmental Psychology*, **41**, 160–170.

Gottlieb, G. (2003). On making behavior genetics truly developmental. *Human Development*, **46**, 337–355.

Hamilton, L. C. (1992). *Regression with graphics: A second course in applied statistics*. Pacific Grove, CA: Brooks/Cole.

Hamilton, L. C. (2006). *Statistics with stata (updated for version 9)*. Pacific Grove: Brooks/Cole.

Jaffee, S. R., Moffitt, T. E., Caspi, A., & Taylor, A. (2003). Life with (or without) father: The benefits of living with two biological parents depend on the father's antisocial behavior. *Child Development*, **73**, 109–126.

Johnson, P. O., & Neyman, J. (1936). Tests of certain linear hypotheses and their applications to some educational problems. *Statistics Research Memoirs*, **1**, 57–93.

Judd, C. M., & Kenny, D. A. (1981a). *Estimating the effects of social interventions*. New York: Cambridge University Press.

Judd, C. M., & Kenny, D. A. (1981b). Process analysis: Estimating mediation in treatment evaluations. *Evaluation Review*, **5**, 602–619.

Kerlinger, F. N., & Pedhazur, E. J. (1973). *Multiple regression in behavioral research*. New York: Holt, Rinehart and Winston.

MacKinnon, D. P., Lockwood, C. M., Hoffman, J. M., West, S. G., & Sheets, V. (2002). A comparison of methods to test mediation and other intervening variable effects. *Psychological Methods*, **7**, 83–104.

MacKinnon, D. P., Lockwood, C. M., & Williams, J. (2004). Confidence limits for the indirect effect: Distribution of the product and resampling methods. *Multivariate Behavioral Research*, **39**, 99–128.

MacKinnon, D. P., Warsi, G., & Dwyer, J. H. (1995). A simulation study of mediated effect measures. *Multivariate Behavioral Research*, **30**, 41–62.

MacKinnon, D. P., Yoon, M., Lockwood, C. M., & Taylor, A. (2005). *A comparison of methods to test mediation and other intervening variable effects in logistic regression*. Unpublished manuscript.

Magnusson, D., & Stattin, H. (1998). Person-context interaction theories. In W. Damon & R. Lerner (Eds.), *Handbook of child psychology: Volume 1: Theoretical models of human development* (5th ed., pp. 685–759). Hoboken, NJ: John Wiley and Sons.

McCartney, K., Dearing, E., & Taylor, B. A. (2003). *Is high-quality child care an intervention for children living in poverty?* Poster presented at the biennial meeting of the Society for Research in Child Development, Tampa, FL.

Muthén, L. K., & Muthén, B. O. (2004). *Mplus user's guide* (3rd ed.). Los Angeles: Authors.

O'Connor, B. P. (1998). All-in-one programs for exploring interactions in moderated multiple regression. *Educational and Psychological Measurement*, **58**, 833–837.

O'Connor, B. P. (2006). *Simple: All-in-one programs for exploring interactions in moderated multiple regression*. http://flash.lakeheadu.ca/~boconno2/simple.html

Parke, R. D., & Buriel, R. (1998). Socialization in the family: Ethnic and ecological perspectives. In W. Damon & N. Eisenberg (Eds.), *Handbook of child psychology: Volume 3: Social, emotional, and personality development* (5th ed., pp. 463–552). Hoboken, NJ: John Wiley & Sons.

Preacher, K. J., Curran, P. J., & Bauer, D. J. (2006). *Probing interactions in multiple linear regression, latent curve analysis, and hierarchical linear modeling: Interactive calculation tools for simple intercepts, simple slopes, and regions of significance*. www.quantpsy.org

Preacher, K. J., Curran, P. J., & Bauer, D. J. (in press). Computational tools for probing interactions in multiple linear regression, multilevel models, and latent curve analysis. *Journal of Educational and Behavioral Statistics*.

Preacher, K. J., & Hayes, A. F. (2004). SPSS and SAS procedures for estimating indirect effects in simple mediation models. *Behavior Research Methods, Instruments, and Computers*, **36**, 717–731.

Preacher, K. J., & Hayes, A. F. (2006). *Asymptotic and re-sampling strategies for assessing and comparing indirect effects in simple and multiple mediator models*. Unpublished manuscript.

Preacher, K. J., & Leonardelli, G. J. (2006). *Calculation for the Sobel test: An interactive calculation tool for mediation tests*. http://www.unc.edu/~preacher/sobel/sobel.htm

Schubert, T., & Jacoby, J. (2004). *SiSSy: Simple slope syntax for test of moderation and simple slopes for one dichotomous or continuous moderator candidate of one centered IV in SPSS.* http://www.igroup.org/projects/sissy/

Shrout, P. E., & Bolger, N. (2002). Mediation in experimental and non-experimental studies: New procedures and recommendations. *Psychological Methods, 7*, 422–445.

Sobel, M. E. (1982). Asymptotic confidence intervals for indirect effects in structural equation models. In S. Leinhardt (Ed.), *Sociological methodology* (pp. 290–312). Washington, DC: American Sociological Association.

Stone, C. A., & Sobel, M. E. (1990). The robustness of estimates of total indirect effects in covariance structure models estimated by maximum likelihood. *Psychometrika, 55*, 337–352.

UCLA Academic Technology Services (2006). *STATA FAQ: How to perform Sobel-Goodman mediation tests in STATA.* http://www.ats.ucla.edu/STAT/stata/faq/sgmediation.htm

VI. SELECTION, DETECTION, AND REFLECTION

SELECTION

Two main questions guide developmental inquiry: What is the typical course of development, and what are the causes of individual differences in development? The first question has been addressed with descriptive statistics (e.g., mean, standard deviation, range, or within-subject longitudinal analyses to describe patterns of change), while the second requires inferential statistics to determine whether associations might exist (e.g., regression analysis or between-subjects longitudinal analyses that identifies factors associated with individual patterns of change). At best, inferential statistics provide a good approximation of truth, as researchers test theories with data. At worst, inferential statistics provide inaccurate information, biasing both future theory and poor decision-making regarding practices and policies for children.

Inferential statistics are used to deduce causal mechanisms in two very different designs. The first is random assignment. In this case, the researcher links a treatment variable, which is randomly assigned to a subsample of participants, with a hypothesized outcome. Random assignment permits causal inference because any initial differences between treatment and control groups, measured and unmeasured, are due solely to chance. Developmentalists can assess causal relations when we randomly assign children to conditions of interest. The second design does not offer the same methodological rigor as the first. For both practical and ethical reasons, nonexperimental, observational, or correlational research designs are more widely used by developmentalists than are randomized experiments. In this case, the researcher attempts to link a treatment variable of interest, which varies naturally among members of a population, with a hypothesized outcome. Of course, one can never infer causality from correlational data because the effect of the treatment variable cannot be isolated from other variables. For this reason, it is more accurate to replace the term "treatment variable" with "predictor variable."

This chapter focuses on omitted variables bias, which arises when one or more variables, related to both the predictor and outcome variables, are not included in the analysis model. Even in the most comprehensive study, some potentially important variables will not have been observed. The influence of unobserved variables may be reflected in estimates of the association between a predictor and outcome—this is a challenge that underlies all nonexperimental research. Economists refer to this as the endogeneity problem because the problem concerns associations within the structure of the data. Developmentalists refer to this problem as selection, that is, non-random assignment into treatment or control groups through self-selection, parental choice, or another mechanism. Historically, economists and methodologists have worried more about potential selection effects than developmentalists (see Heckman, 1979).

The purpose of this chapter is to provide developmentalists with an overview of methods that have been developed to address selection bias, many of which are seldom used in developmental research. There is a technical literature on this topic that has not, for the most part, influenced developmental practice. As a result, developmental research is often dismissed by social scientists from other disciplines. This overview, like other chapters in this monograph, does not offer a technical discussion of methodological issues, although we refer interested readers to this literature. Instead, it is a user-friendly, how-to guide to get researchers started and to encourage reflective practice. We hope developmentalists will add these techniques to their toolbox of statistical methods.

DETECTION

In this section, we review five modeling strategies that have been used to detect associations between predictor and outcome variables in nonexperimental research: regression with covariates, propensity score analysis, instrumental variables analysis, fixed effects analysis, and regression discontinuity. We recognize that regression with covariates is a familiar technique to most developmentalists and we include it in this chapter solely as a comparison against which other less familiar techniques can be contrasted. The strategies to address selection vary widely, from liberal to conservative. Table 1 displays each of the modeling strategies, their purpose, their primary assumptions, and the corresponding statistical packages and commands. For illustrative purposes, we provide an example of four of the five strategies using data from the National Institute of Child Health and Human Development Study of Early Child Care and Youth Development (NICHD SECCYD), a longitudinal study of children from 1 month through 15 years (for a description of the study, see NICHD Early Child Care Research Network, 2005). We are not able to illustrate the fifth strategy

TABLE I

MODELING STRATEGIES, PURPOSES, PRIMARY ASSUMPTIONS, AND CORRESPONDING STATISTICAL PACKAGES FOR ADDRESSING SELECTION BIAS IN STATISTICAL ANALYSES

Technique	Assumptions	Sources of Bias Accounted For	Possible Problems	Program	Command
Regression with a *simple* and *comprehensive* set of covariates	(1) The relation between the predictor and outcome is linear; (2) the residuals are uncorrelated with the predictors in the model	Covariates included if modeled correctly	Biased estimation and potential overcontrol if directionality is ignored	Standard statistical packages such as SAS, STATA, and SPSS	The command is **proc mixed** in SAS, **xtmixed** in STATA, and **regression** in SPSS
Propensity score analysis	(1) Selection is on the observables and thus there are no omitted variables that influence both the treatment and the outcome; (2) predictors directly affect the treatment but not the outcomes for different groups	Accounts for variables included in propensity analysis–ensures modeling is correct	Does not adjust for omitted variables	The most appropriate package is STATA	The command is **pscore** in STATA
Instrumental variables analysis	(1) The instrument is correlated with the predictor for which it is an instrument; (2) instrument affects the outcome only through the treatment; and (3) instrument must be uncorrelated with residuals in second stage	Measured and omitted variables	Reduced power and problems identifying instrumental variables	The most appropriate package is STATA.	The command is **ivreg** in STATA

Table 1. (Contd.)

Technique	Assumptions	Sources of Bias Accounted For	Possible Problems	Program	Command
Fixed effect analysis	(1) The relation between the predictor and outcome is linear; (2) the residuals are uncorrelated with the predictors in the model	Included variables if modeled correctly and Omitted variables have some impact over time	Reduced statistical powers	Standard statistical packages such as SAS, STATA and SPSS	The command is **xtreg** in STATA, **proc mixed** in SAS, and **analyze glm or analyze mixed models** in SPSS
Regression discontinuity analysis	(1) The distribution of the pre–post test scores is best described as a polynomial function;(2) the two groups come from a single continuous pretest distribution and division between the groups is determined by a cutoff; and (3) treatment is administered uniformly	Measured and omitted variables	Large sample sizes required to detect even small effects	Standard statistical packages such as SAS, STATA and SPSS	The command is **proc mixed** in SAS, **xtmixed** in STATA, and **regression** in SPSS

(regression discontinuity analysis) with the NICHD SECCYD data because our predictor of interest (i.e., maternal occupational prestige) is not an appropriate treatment variable for this method; instead, we refer readers to several examples from the literature.

We have chosen to test the hypothesis that children's math achievement is associated with mothers' higher occupational status. Note, however, that a researcher would prefer to test a causal hypothesis, namely that children's math achievement is enhanced when mothers have higher occupational status. Occupational status was coded using a 13-point occupational scale, where 1 denotes the highest prestige. Math achievement was assessed with the Woodcock–Johnson Applied Problems subscale. For three of the modeling strategies (regression with covariates, propensity score analysis, and instrumental variables analysis), we used maternal occupational prestige at third grade to predict children's third grade math scores; for the fourth strategy (fixed-effects analysis), we modeled changes in math scores between 54 months and fifth grade as a function of changes in maternal occupational status during this period. Our purpose here is not to answer a substantive question of interest. Rather, our purpose is to test a hypothesis to illustrate the method and to demonstrate how the answer may vary across model specifications. We begin with an important caveat from Winship and Morgan (1999): "No one statistical model is a panacea" (p. 695). A researcher's choice should depend upon a careful consideration of the research question, characteristics of the data set, potential confounding variables, and whether the data are up to the task at hand (e.g., Do the data meet the model assumptions? Is there enough power to detect an association? Is there sufficient variability in the predictor and outcome?).

Regression With Covariates

This is the most commonly used modeling technique to address selection issues in developmental science. The logic is relatively simple. A researcher strives to control for potential third variables, or mediators, by including a set of covariates in the regression model. In so doing, one attempts to isolate the influence of a predictor of interest. Two important assumptions underlie this model. First, the relation between the predictor and the outcome is linear. The second assumption is harder to grasp but worth the effort. It concerns the residuals, that is, the difference between predicted scores on the regression line and the actual scores for each individual; these residuals tell us how much error there is in our prediction. When the influence of the predictor is great, the observed scores more closely approximate the predicted scores, and the residuals are smaller. When a researcher adds a predictor, the residuals typically decrease because one accounts for more variance in the outcome. Regression analysis assumes that the predictor is uncorrelated with the residuals (i.e., the error term). When this condition is met, the residuals, large or small, reflect other variables that are unrelated to the treatment. When this condition is not met, then we have a biased estimate of the predictor because the association reflects both the predictor and other variables, observed or unobserved.

Using the NICHD data set, we first regressed the outcome, children's math scores at third grade, on the predictor, maternal occupational status at third grade. Then, we regressed children's math scores on the predictor, as well as a set of control variables: gender (male), child birth order, maternal education, maternal sensitivity, maternal depression, partner status, partner education, partner income, and classroom quality. Why these controls? The answer to this question can only be found in the developmental literature. Children's math achievement has, in fact, been linked with gender, birth order, characteristics of mothers, and schooling. By controlling for these variables, we in essence attempt to rule out rival hypotheses to the hypothesis of interest, which in this case concerns maternal occupational status as a predictor. A sample regression equation is presented in Table 2.

There was evidence that maternal occupational status predicted children's math scores at third grade (see Table 3). Specifically, in a model that only included our predictor variable, children whose mothers had more prestigious occupations (i.e., lower values) had higher math scores than children whose mothers had less prestigious occupations ($B = -1.16$, $p < .001$). This B essentially provides the same information as r but r is standardized, while B is in the units of the outcome, in this case math scores. Next, in an effort to control for potential third variables, we added to the model the set of covariates described above. Maternal occupational status remained a statistically significant predictor of children's math scores at third grade. Examination of the Bs across models showed that the effect size of the predictor of interest dropped by more than half when the covariates were added to the model. Note, also, that some of the covariates were statistically significant as well. All statistical packages include commands for regression analysis, and they are all comparable.

In nonexperimental work, researchers attempt to model all important sources of influence from an infinite set of experiences. When models fail to include a key variable as identified from the relevant literature, they can fairly be criticized as under controlled. The size of the data set can constrain the number of predictors. A good guideline is one predictor for every 10 participants. Violation of this guideline can result in overfitting, such that the results tend not to be generalizable from the sample to the population (Tabachnick & Fidell, 1996). With a large data set, researchers have the luxury of fitting models with numerous covariates as well as with a more limited set of variables. For example, Fryer and Levitt (2004) demonstrated that the achievement gap between black and white children can be

110

TABLE 2

SAMPLE EQUATIONS AND CORRESPONDING DESCRIPTION OF THE COMPONENTS FOR EACH MODELING STRATEGY

	Equations	Explanation
Regression with a *comprehensive* set of covariates	$Y_i = \beta_0 + \beta_1 X_i + \beta_2 Z_i$	Y_i is the outcome for individual I β_1 is the effect of predictor of interest, controlling for all other covariates X_i is the predictor of interest Z_i is a vector of covariates
Propensity score analysis	Step 1: $T_i = \lambda_0 + \lambda_1 X_1 + \lambda_2 X_2 + \dots \lambda_m X_n + \delta_i$ Step 2: $Y_i = \beta_0 + \beta_1 T_i + \beta_2 P_1 + \beta_3 P_2 + \dots \beta_m P_n + \varepsilon_i$	*Step 1* T_i is the outcome in logistic regression analysis (treatment) X_1, X_2, etc. are selection variables identified from the literature *Step 2* Y_i is the outcome for individual I β_1 is the effect of predictor of interest, controlling for the propensity blocks T_i is the treatment effect P_1, P_2, etc. represent matched groups within a given propensity block
Instrumental variables analysis	Stage 1: $T_i = \lambda_0 + \lambda_1 \text{INS} + \lambda_3 Z_i + \delta_i$ Stage 2: $Y_i = \beta_0 + \beta_1 {}^\wedge T_i + \gamma Z_i + \varepsilon_i$	*Stage 1* T_i is the first stage outcome (treatment) λ_1 is the coefficient on the instrument (INS) Z_i is a vector of covariates *Stage 2* Y_i is the outcome for individual i β_1 is the causal effect of treatment ${}^\wedge T_i$ is the predicted value of the treatment from the first stage equation X_i is a vector of covariates

Table 2. (Contd.)

	Equations	Explanation
Fixed effect analysis	$Y_{ij} = \beta_0 + \beta_1 \text{Age}_{ij} + \beta_2 T_{ij} + (\gamma_1 I_1 + \gamma_2 I_2 + \dots \gamma_n I_n) + \beta_3 Z_i + \varepsilon_I$	Y_{ij} is the outcome at two levels $\gamma_1 I_1$, etc. are dummy variables representing the fixed effects of individuals; in a random effects model, these terms would be reflected in the U_i error term T_{ij} is the time-varying treatment variable (i.e., maternal occupational prestige) Age_{ij} is the individual's age Z_i is a vector of covariates
Regression discontinuity analysis	$Y_i = \beta_0 + \beta_1 T_i + \gamma(X_i - X_c) + \varepsilon_i$	Y_i is the outcome for individual i β_1 is the causal effect of treatment T_i is a dichotomous variable representing treatment assignment $X_i - X_c$ is the exogenous covariate used to determine treatment centered on the cutoff point

Note. — β_0 and λ_0 represent the individual's value on the outcome when all other variables are 0.

112

TABLE 3

RESULTS FROM REGRESSION WITH COVARIATES ANALYSES FOR CHILDREN'S MATH SCORES AT THIRD GRADE

	Math Scores	
	Third Grade ($n = 741$)	
	Model 1	Model 2
Maternal occupation status	− 1.16 (.169)***	− .429 (.190)*
Male (1 month)		.997 (.861)
Birth order (1 month)		− .961 (.479)*
Maternal employment hours		− .008 (.035)
Maternal education (1 month)		.942 (.249)***
Maternal sensitivity		1.76 (.603)**
Maternal depression		− .037 (.050)
Partner education (1 month)		.319 (.225)
Partner income (square root)		.006 (.008)
Classroom quality		.576 (.572)
R^2	.078	.205

***$p < .001$. **$p < .01$. *$p < .05$.

explained nearly as well by a parsimonious set of family controls ($n = 9$ predictors) as by a much larger set ($n > 100$ predictors). Researchers can perhaps have greater confidence in their findings when the estimate is robust across model specifications.

It is also possible to overcontrol in an attempt to model associations among variables. Newcombe (2003) warns that when researchers suppress the effect of one predictor to model the effect of a correlated treatment, the results may be misleading. She argues that "not all factors that initially seem to be confounding 'background factors' should be statistically controlled if the aim is to understand the lives of families" (p. 1050). Her point is that one cannot remove the effect of one variable from another if it cannot be removed in real life. As an example, Newcombe questioned whether one could sensibly remove maternal income and maternal depression when modeling the effect of maternal employment on child outcomes, as we have done here, given that maternal employment increases income and decreases depression. She reminds the field of an important lesson: theory and conceptualization must guide model building. It is important to remember that statistical control is a means of identifying relations, other things being equal—of course, other things are typically not equal.

For those interested in learning more about multiple regression analysis, we refer you to a text by Tabachnick and Fidell (1996) and a technical chapter by Rubinfeld (2000).

This is a relatively new statistical technique, developed by Rubin (1978) to address selection bias. The term propensity refers to a conditional probability of an individual being in a treatment group, given a set of background variables for that individual. In step 1, logistic regression is used to predict treatment versus control status from a set of background variables identified by the researcher. Logistic regression relies on weaker assumptions than other regression techniques, and, as such, propensity score analysis tends to be considerably more robust to model misspecification (Drake, 1993). Propensity score analysis does have assumptions. Specifically, there can be no omitted variables that influence both the predictor of interest and the outcome; in other words, propensity score analysis cannot really solve the problem of omitted variables bias. In addition, the predictors of treatment cannot also differentially influence the outcomes of the treated and untreated groups.

From the logistic regression, each participant receives a single propensity score, that is, the probability of being in a given group, for example an intervention program. Children receiving the intervention should have high propensity scores based on the set of background variables. Children with similar background characteristics who were eligible for the intervention but were not in the intervention should also have high propensity scores. Thus, propensity score analysis can be used to identify a suitable comparison group to the treatment. Of course, researchers can never be assured that they have identified all background variables that influenced selection into a given treatment; economists would say that the treatment in not exogenous in a nonexperimental design.

In step 2, researchers use the propensity scores to test hypotheses about the predictor of interest. Two strategies are typically used. First, one can enter the continuous propensity score in a regression equation to control for selection factors; however, it is not clear that there is any advantage of doing this other than saving degrees of freedom. Entering a vector of family background variables controls for selection effects about as well as entering a single propensity score. Second, researchers can use propensity scores to create matched groups: treated and untreated. Statistical programs typically allow you to specify the number of propensity blocks or subgroups, from high to low propensity of being treated. The blocks will be comprised of matched groups, generated through an iterative process. The groups are matched in that the mean values for all covariates within a block will be approximately the same for the treated and untreated groups. The two groups within a block can then be compared on outcome variables of interest using a variety of inferential statistics, ranging from the *t*-test to longitudinal models. Note that although we do not demonstrate this here, it is also possible to fit separate regression models within each propensity block and then average the coefficients across models to obtain a mean treatment effect. Researchers tend to make stronger claims regarding treatment effects using matched samples than when using multiple regression with covariates, although some would question the logic of this. Of course, it is possible that a suitable number of comparison individuals will not exist within a data set of interest, in which case propensity score analysis cannot be conducted. It is also possible that participants will not be matched on unobserved factors, an advantage of random assignment. We provide sample equations for both steps in Table 2.

To illustrate the propensity score technique, we return to our working example of the association between maternal occupational status and children's math scores. We begin by dichotomizing maternal occupational status, such that mothers who were in occupations classified as executive or professional received a score of 1 and mothers with other levels of occupational status received a score of 0. As such, our predictor of interest was professional occupational status. Next, we examined descriptive statistics for the two groups (i.e., professional occupation and other occupation) on the family background variables. Then, using logistic regression, we predicted the probability of being in a professional occupation from the set of family background variables, and each individual received a propensity score. We obtained six matched blocks, that is, blocks in which individuals were equally likely to be in a professional occupation as not, given similar background characteristics. As a final step, we fitted two regression models: the first with the continuous propensity score as a control and the second with the six matched blocks as controls.

We began by examining descriptive statistics on the covariates for mothers whose occupational status was classified as professional and for mothers of other occupational status. Mothers in the professional sample were more educated than other mothers ($M = 16.22$ vs. 13.45 years), were less depressed ($M = 7.25$ vs. 9.72), had partners with more education ($M = 15.84$ vs. 13.76 years), and a higher annual income ($M = \$58,250$ vs. $\$39,621$). The two groups did not differ significantly on the remaining family characteristics. Next, we used the continuous propensity score as a control variable in a regression model predicting children's math scores at third grade from maternal professional occupational status at third grade (Table 4). Professional occupational status was not a significant predictor of children's math scores at third grade ($B = 1.42$, $p > .10$). Not surprisingly the propensity to be in a professional occupation (i.e., the single linear vector of covariates) was positively and significantly associated with math scores in third grade.

In the final model, we replaced the continuous propensity score with five dummy variables representing the six matched propensity blocks

TABLE 4

RESULTS FROM PROPENSITY SCORE ANALYSES FOR CHILDREN'S MATH
SCORES AT THIRD GRADE

	Math Scores	
	Continuous Propensity Score	Matched Propensity Blocks
Professional occupation	1.42 (1.20)	1.81 (1.22)
Continuous propensity score	11.55 (2.06)***	
Propensity block 2		1.15 (1.33)
Propensity block 3		4.87 (1.94)*
Propensity block 4		5.48 (1.65)**
Propensity block 5		8.56 (1.98)***
Propensity block 6		7.85 (2.36)**
R^2	.097	.090

***$p < .001$. **$p < .01$. *$p < .05$.

(Table 4). Again, professional occupational status was not a significant predictor of children's math scores at third grade ($B = 1.81, p > .10$); this is the test of the association between our predictor of interest and children's third grade math scores. An examination of the Bs for each propensity block showed that higher propensity blocks (i.e., blocks with propensity scores .40 or greater) significantly predicted children's math scores at third grade, while lower propensity blocks (i.e., $< .40$) did not.

For those interested in learning more about propensity score analysis, we refer you to technical articles by D'Agostino (1998), Rosenbaum and Rubin (1983), and Rubin (1997). Applications of propensity score analysis can be found in Harding (2003) and Hill, Waldfogel, Brooks-Gunn, and Han (2005).

Instrumental Variables Analysis

To use this technique, researchers must identify an instrument, that is, an exogenous variable that is directly related to the predictor and indirectly related to the outcome through the predictor. Instrumental variable analysis is a two-stage process and is typically fitted using two-stage least squares estimation. In the first stage, the predictor is regressed on the instrument as well as any other controls to produce predicted values of the predictor. In the second stage, the outcome is regressed on the predicted scores for the predictor of interest, based on the instrument, as well as any other controls, to produce an unbiased estimate of the treatment effect on the outcome. Because the instrument cannot be directly correlated with the outcome, one controls statistically for omitted variables bias by relying on the instrument as a predictor. See Table 2 for examples of first and second stage equations.

We searched for an instrument for maternal occupational prestige in the NICHD SECCYD data set. For example, we considered a geo-coded variable, percent professional education within a census block. Satisfying the first assumption, this instrument was correlated with our predictor of interest ($r = -.29$, $p < .001$). However, the instrument was both directly ($r = .21$, $p < .001$) and indirectly related to the outcome (Note: we also predicted third grade math scores from the predictor and the instrument and the instrument remained a significant predictor, $B = .17$, $p < .001$). As such, percent professional education within a census block did not meet the assumptions of this technique. We fitted the instrumental variables model anyway and as predicted maternal occupational status (derived from the first stage analysis) was not a significant predictor of third-grade math scores, controlling for the set of family covariates used in other models.

Other researchers have been more fortunate in identifying an instrument. Foster and McLanahan (1996) used city labor market characteristics as an instrument for neighborhood high school drop-out rate to model high school completion. Hoxby (2000) used natural boundaries of metropolitan areas (e.g., rivers) as an instrument for school choice to model school achievement. And Angrist and Krueger (1999) used quarter of an individual's birth (e.g., January through March, and so on) as an instrument for years of educational attainment to model labor market earnings. Papers that use instrumental variables analysis usually generate controversy in the field about the appropriateness of the instrument.

For those interested in learning more, we refer you to additional technical articles by Angrist, Imbens, and Rubin (1996), Doran (1989), and Duncan and Raudenbush (under review).

Fixed Effects Analysis

Fixed effects can be used when the study design includes repeated measures of the predictor and the outcome. Essentially, this approach involves replacing observed values with difference scores for all predictor and outcome variables to correct for omitted variables bias. The main assumption of this technique is that omitted variables as well as predictors of interest have similar impacts at all time points. If this is true, then using difference scores results in the removal of omitted variables bias because their influence is subtracted out (consider that time-1 and time-2 variables both include the effect of omitted variables). A technical way of explaining this is that fixed-effects controls for unobserved subject-level heterogeneity that may bias the relation between the predictor and the outcome. Another important assumption is that any omitted variables have only main effects on the predictor and the outcomes (Greene, 1997). When these assumptions are met, fixed effects analysis provides a very powerful test of causality for nonexperimental data; it is also a very conservative test (Levy & Duncan, 2001). It is worth noting that any repeated-measures analysis is prone to bias when the ability to measure the outcome varies over time (Bryk & Weisburg, 1977). Further, when the repeated measures are highly correlated, precision is lost. It is critical for researchers to ask whether their data meet these assumptions before using fixed-effects analysis.

To examine the association between maternal occupational status and children's math scores using fixed-effects analysis, we fitted a longitudinal model in which we predicted change in math scores between 54 months and fifth grade from change in maternal occupational status during this time period (see Table 2 for an example equation). Grade, centered at kindergarten, served as the time variable and all interactions between grade and the covariates were computed. Because math scores were nested within children (i.e., each child has multiple math assessments), our repeated factor was the individual. In the first model, child-specific residuals were treated as random effects. In other words, we assumed that all predictors varied randomly (i.e., differences across individuals are not fixed and are due to sources one cannot identify); as such, the error-term consisted of both within-individual residuals (i.e., deviation of the predicted score from the actual score) and between-individual residuals (i.e., deviation of each child's mean from the grand mean). In the second model, child-specific residuals were treated as fixed effects. In other words, the between-individual residuals (i.e., differences across individuals) were essentially removed from the error term and included as a series of predictors (in this case dummy variables representing each individual) in the regression equation. In a fixed-effects model, all time-invariant effects such as child gender or birth order are necessarily dropped from the regression model, thereby controlling for all stable characteristics of the individual —observed and unobserved. This is because the child-level fixed effects explain all possible child-level differences in the outcome variable. Note, however, that interactions between time-invariant predictors and time may be retained.

Because fixed-effects analysis relies on change, we began by examining the within-individual variability in maternal occupational status between 54 months and fifth grade. Correlation coefficients ranged from a low of .53 to a high of .80, suggesting that there was limited variability in maternal occupational status. As such, our power to detect an effect using fixed-effects analysis may have been compromised. Again, for illustrative purposes, we fit the model anyway and, not surprisingly, change in maternal occupational status was not a statistically significant predictor of change in children's math scores between kindergarten and fifth grade. Results from these analyses can be found in Table 5. Thus, this conservative test provides no evidence for an association between maternal occupational status and

TABLE 5

RESULTS FROM FIXED EFFECTS REGRESSION ANALYSIS FOR MATH OUTCOMES BETWEEN
54 MONTHS AND FIFTH GRADE

	Math scores	
	Fixed Effects for Individuals ($n = 836$)	
	Model 1	Model 2
Maternal occupation status	− .417 (.142)**	− .014 (.187)
Maternal occupation status × grade	.114 ((.033)***	− .001 (.048)
Grade	21.50 (.242)***	28.22 (2.08)***
Grade^2	− 1.98 (.044)***	− 2.88 (.446)***
Maternal employment hours		− .036 (.031)
Maternal sensitivity		− .200 (.478)
Maternal sensitivity × grade		− .957 (.336)**
Maternal sensitivity × grade^2		.212 (.077)**
Maternal depression		.008 (.046)
Partner income (square root)		.004 (007)
Classroom quality		077 (050)
Variance components		
σ_U	13.67	13.08
σ_e	9.10	8.91

***$p < .001$. **$p < .01$. *$p < .05$.

children's math scores. SAS and Stata offer the two most user-friendly statistical packages for fixed-effects analysis.

For those interested in learning more about fixed-effects analysis, we
refer you to a book by Allison (1990) and a technical article by Greene
(1997). Applications of fixed-effects analysis can be found in Rivkin,
Hanushek, and Kain (2005) and NICHD Early Child Care Research
Network and Duncan (2003).

Comparison of Findings Across Fitted Models

A comparison of findings across the four modeling strategies reveals
that the more conservative techniques (propensity score analysis, instrumental variables analysis, and fixed effects analysis) failed to detect an association between maternal occupational status and children's math scores,
while the more liberal technique (regression with covariates) resulted in a
significant association. Note, however, that we failed to identify a good instrument for the instrumental variables analysis and that the relative stability of maternal occupational status may have compromised the fixed-
effects analysis. We offered these findings for illustrative purposes only and
not to answer a substantive question of interest. It is, of course, difficult to

119

know what the "truth" is when findings are not robust across modeling techniques, although clearly one can have more confidence in the findings for more conservative models. This should be sobering to developmentalists, who have tended to rely on more liberal techniques.

Regression Discontinuity Analysis

This technique is one of the most powerful designs for detecting causal effects in nonexperimental studies (Cook & Campbell, 1979). It relies on the identification of a variable that is related to a predictor of interest in a discontinuous way. More specifically, individuals are assigned to a treatment or control group based solely on a threshold for a given predictor—everyone above the threshold is assigned to one group (e.g., treatment) and everyone below the threshold is assigned to another (e.g., control). For example, children's pretest reading scores (the predictor) might be used to determine whether or not a child receives remedial services (the treatment); all children above the cut point would not receive services while all children below the score would receive remedial services. Because assignment to treatment is known rather than unknown (Pitts, Prost, & Winters, 2004), the regression discontinuity design essentially compares the outcomes of individuals who receive a treatment with those who do not. In essence, the researcher can identify the causal impact of the variable of interest simply by comparing individuals who scored just above the cutoff with individuals who scored just below the cutoff. In the case of our example, the outcomes of children just below the cutoff who received remedial services would be compared with the outcomes of children just above the cutoff who did not receive remedial services. Any differences could presumably be attributed to the treatment (i.e., remedial services). As such, one of the benefits of regression discontinuity analysis is that some of the ethical concerns of experimental research are avoided because assignment to the treatment condition is not manipulated experimentally.

There are two types of regression discontinuity designs: sharp and fuzzy. In a sharp regression discontinuity design, treatment is determined solely by some observable characteristic (like a cutoff score on a pretest). This characteristic is identified by the researcher and is the only thing that determines whether or not an individual receives the treatment. Under these circumstances, one's ability to make causal inferences approaches that of a randomized experiment (Bloom, Kemple, Gamse, & Jacob, 2005). In a fuzzy regression discontinuity design, treatment may be determined by one or more unknown characteristics but the conditional probability of receiving the treatment is discontinuous at the cutpoint (Hahn, Todd, & Van der Klaauw, 2001). A fuzzy design requires a larger range of data to maintain precision. For both designs, average treatment effects can only be identified precisely at the point where the probability of receiving the treatment changes discontinuously (i.e., the cutoff point). That is, the range of scores for which a treatment effect can be identified is relatively narrow and clustered around the cutpoint for assignment to the two groups (Hahn et al., 2001).

In the first step of a regression discontinuity analysis, the researcher determines what pretest cutoff score or threshold will be used and what group will receive the treatment (those above or below the threshold). In the second step, regression analysis is used to predict a posttest score from a dichotomous treatment variable (i.e., above or below the cutoff), as well as from the pretest score, centered around the cutoff score, and any other covariates. The pretest score is centered around the cutoff score so that the intercept is equal to the cutoff score. In this analysis the coefficient for the treatment variable represents an unbiased estimate of the treatment on the outcome. See Table 2 for a sample regression discontinuity equation.

Regression discontinuity analysis has several assumptions. First, unobserved characteristics of an individual must vary continuously with the observed characteristic used to identify the cutoff (Jacobs & Lefgren, 2002). Second, the treatment and control groups must both come from a single continuous pretest distribution and the division between groups must be determined by a cutoff. Finally, the distribution of pretest and posttest scores must be described with a polynomial function. In other words, the relationship between the outcome variable and the test score used to determine treatment must be linear, quadratic, cubic, etc., on both sides of the cutoff. In addition to these assumptions, regression discontinuity relies on the fact that the cutoff score is followed without exception and that the treatment program is administered uniformly to all participants. When these assumptions and requirements are met, regression discontinuity analysis provides one of the most powerful tests of causality in nonexperimental data. It is worth noting that despite the strengths of regression discontinuity, there are also limitations. In particular, a researcher must have a sample size that is two or three times the sample size needed in a randomized experiment in order to detect comparable effects (Pitts et al., 2004). This is due in part to the narrow range of scores for which a treatment effect can be detected.

Although we are unable to illustrate this technique with our sample data because the predictor of interest (i.e., maternal occupational prestige) was not an appropriate treatment variable, we offer several examples of research that have successfully employed regression discontinuity analysis. Gormley, Gayer, Phillips, and Dawson (2005) used the exogenous variation generated by state-mandated age cutoffs for entering school to identify the impact of prekindergarten programs on children's outcomes. More specifically, the authors compare the outcomes of kindergarten children who attended prekindergarten in the previous year (i.e., the marginal treatment group) with the outcomes of children who were just enrolling in prekindergarten

121

because they missed the age cutoff for prekindergarten (i.e., the marginal control group). The authors identified positive effects of prekindergarten attendance on children's achievement outcomes. Jacobs and Lefgren (2002) examined the impact of summer school on students' math and reading skills by assigning students to summer school based on pretest measures of reading and math and then comparing posttest reading and math scores of the treatment and control groups. The authors found that summer school increased children's subsequent reading and mathematics scores. Angrist and Lavy (1999) used a maximum enrollment rule, which stipulates a new classroom be added when average class size exceeds a threshold, to assess the impact of class size on student test scores. Students were assigned to smaller classes when enrollment reached 41 and student achievement was compared for students under alternative assignments of class size. The authors found that reducing class size results in a significant increase in student test scores.

For those interested in learning more, we refer you to additional technical articles by Hahn et al. (2001); Shadish, Cook, and Campbell (2002); and Thistlethwaite and Campbell (1960).

REFLECTION

We conclude this brief overview by offering three pieces of advice. First, take the problem of selection bias seriously. Statisticians define selection bias as "nonignorable treatment assignment." Unfortunately, too often nonrandom treatment assignment is all but ignored in developmental research. Because the goal of social science research is to test hypotheses as rigorously as possible, developmentalists need to address the issue of selection bias more seriously, and more rigorously, in our work—otherwise it is our work that will be ignored. It is worth mentioning that no technique can address all sources of bias with complete assurance in nonexperimental designs. For this reason, methodologists have often implored social scientists to consider using experimental designs. Of course, there are often either practical or ethical limitations that prevent true experimentation. For example, experiments often involve costs associated with treatment, a practical constraint; in addition, experiments may call for subjecting children to risks or withholding treatments, both ethical constraints (Cook & Payne, 2002).

Quasi-experiments or natural experiments offer another important alternative to nonexperimental designs, for example, studies of policies that result in treatment change. The value of naturally occurring treatments over which participants have no control is that they offer a nonbiased treatment, free of selection effects. There are a number of excellent examples in developmental science of naturally occurring treatments, including Head

Start funding policies (Ludwig & Miller, 2004), the introduction of television to a community (Joy, Kimball, & Zabrack, 1986), and the influx of wealth to Native Americans following the opening of a casino (Costello, Compton, Keeler, & Angold, 2003). Perhaps, Duncan, Magnuson, and Ludwig (2004) are correct that "researchers' first instincts for gathering data should not be to exploit variability in risk, protective, and other contextual measures of interest gathered from convenient homogeneous or even population samples" (p. 75).

Second, Winship and Morgan (1999) advise that "a variety of methods should be implemented to determine how robust the treatment effect estimate is to alternative methods" (p. 703). We agree, which is why we have modeled this approach here. Sometimes, the research question or the structure of the data lends itself to one strategy over another. Often, however, one strategy is not more appropriate. More and more, researchers are not relying on one strategy alone to test a given hypothesis. For example, Hill et al. (2005) modeled the impact of maternal employment patterns on children's cognitive outcomes using propensity score analysis and instrumental variables. The NICHD Early Child Care Research Network, in collaboration with Duncan (2003), modeled child-care quality effects on children's cognitive outcomes using multiple regression with covariates, as well as fixed-effects analysis. And Magnuson, Ruhm, and Waldfogel (2004) modeled the effect of prekindergarten on school readiness using regression, instrumental variables, and propensity score analysis. In all three examples, comparisons across models are illustrative. It is worth noting that the use of different statistical techniques is only one of many factors that a researcher must consider when examining individual differences in an outcome. Just as a statistical technique with more stringent assumptions may lead to more conservative findings, so too can the inclusion (or exclusion) of confounding variables or the specification of a given model.

Our third piece of advice is to take time for reflection. From the construction of a research question to the specification of a model to the examination of the statistical output, we need to think carefully about our logic. For those of us who prefer relying on data to armchair empiricism, it is critical for the data to add value to argument (McCartney & Weiss, 2006). A careful consideration of selection bias needs to be an important part of any nonexperimental study, especially if the data are to lead to warranted conclusions.

ACKNOWLEDGMENT

This project was funded by a Grant from the National Institute of Child Health and Human Development (NICHD) Study of Early Child Care and

Youth Development to the first (HD25451) and third authors. We thank the investigators in the NICHD Early Child Care Research Network for the data set, Eric Dearing for his helpful comments on an earlier draft of this manuscript, the site coordinators and research assistants for their data collection efforts, and the families and teachers for their participation in this longitudinal study.

REFERENCES

Allison, P. D. (1990). Change scores as dependent variables in regression analysis. In C. C. Clogg (ed.), *Sociological methodology, 1990* (pp. 93–114). Washington, DC: American Sociological Association.

Angrist, J. D., Imbens, G. W., & Rubin, D. B. (1996). Identification of causal effects using instrumental variables. *Journal of the American Statistical Association*, **91**, 444–472.

Angrist, J. D., & Krueger, A. (1999). Empirical strategies in labor economics. In O. Ashenfelter & D. Cards (Eds.), *Handbook of labor economics* (Vol. 3a, pp. 1278–1329). Amsterdam: Elsevier Science.

Angrist, J. D., & Lavy, V. (1999). Using maimonides rule to estimate the effect of class size on scholastic achievement. *Quarterly Journal of Economics*, **114**, 535–575.

Bloom, H. S., Kemple, J., Gamse, B., & Jacob, R. (April, 2005). *Using regression discontinuity analysis to measure the impacts of reading first*. Paper presented at the annual meeting of the American Educational Research Association, Montreal, Canada.

Bryk, A., & Weisburg, H. (1977). Use of nonequivalent control group design when subjects are growing. *Psychological Bulletin*, **84**, 950–962.

Cook, T. D., & Campbell, D. T. (1979). *Quasi-experimentation: Design and analysis issues for field settings*. Boston: Houghton Mifflin.

Cook, T. D., & Payne, M. R. (2002). Objecting to the objections to using random assignment in educational research. In F. Mosteller & R. F. Boruch (Eds.), *Evidence matters: Randomized trials in education research* (150–178). Washington, DC: Brookings Institute Press.

Costello, E. J., Compton, S. N., Keeler, G., & Angold, A. (2003). Relationships between poverty and psychopathology: A natural experiment. *Journal of the American Medical Association*, **290**, 2023–2029.

D'Agostino, R. B. (1998). Tutorial in biostatistics: Propensity score methods for bias reduction in the comparison of a treatment to a non-randomized control group. *Statistics in Medicine*, **17**, 2265–2281.

Doran, H. E. (1989). *Applied regression analysis in econometrics*. New York: Marcel Dekker Inc.

Drake, C. (1993). Effects of misspecification of the propensity score on estimators of treatment effect. *Biometrics*, **49**, 1231–1236.

Duncan, G. J., Magnuson, K. A., & Ludwig, J. (2004). The endogeneity problem in developmental studies. *Research in Human Development*, **1** (1 & 2), 59–80.

Duncan, G. J., & Raudenbush, S. W. (under review). *Neighborhoods and adolescent development: How can we determine the links?* Working Paper No. 59.

Foster, E. M., & McClanahan, S. (1996). An illustration of the use of instrumental variables: Do neighborhood conditions affect a young person's chance of finishing high school. *Psychological Methods*, **1** (3), 249–260.

Fryer, R. G., & Levitt, S. D. (2004). Understanding the black–white test score gap in the first two years of school. *The Review of Economics and Statistics*, **86** (2), 447–464.

124

Gormley, W. T., Gayer, T., Phillips, D. A., & Dawson, B. (2005). The effects of universal pre-k on cognitive development. *Developmental Psychology*, **41**, 872–884.

Greene, W. T. (1997). *Econometric analysis*. New Jersey: Prentice-Hall Inc.

Hahn, J., Todd, P., & Van der Klaauw, W. (2001). Identification and estimation of treatment effects with a regression-discontinuity design. *Econometrica*, **69**, 201–209.

Harding, D. J. (2003). Counterfactual models of neighborhood effects: The effect of neighborhood poverty on dropping out and teenage pregnancy. *American Journal of Sociology*, **109** (3), 676–719.

Heckman, J. J. (1979). Sample selection bias as a specification error. *Econometrica*, **47**, 153–161.

Hill, J. L., Waldfogel, J., Brooks Gunn, J., & Han, W. (2005). Maternal employment and child development: A fresh look using newer methods. *Developmental Psychology*, **41**, 833–850.

Hoxby, C. M. (2000). Does competition among public schools benefit students and taxpayers. *The American Economic Review*, **99** (5), 1209–1238.

Jacobs, B. A., & Lefgren, L. (2002). *Remedial Education and Student Achievement: A Regression Discontinuity Analysis*. NBER Working Paper #8918.

Joy, L. A., Kimball, M. M., & Zabrack, M. L. (1986). Television and children's aggressive behavior. In T. M. Williams (ed.), *The impact of television: A natural experiment in three communities* (pp. 303–360). New York: Academic Press.

Levy, D., & Duncan, G. (2001). *Using siblings to assess the effect of childhood income on completed schooling*. Joint Center for Poverty Research, Working Paper, Northwestern University.

Ludwig, J. O., & Miller, D. (2004). *Does Head Start Improve Long-Term Outcomes? Evidence from a Regression Discontinuity Design*. Institute for Research on Poverty, Discussion paper no. 1311–1305.

Magnuson, K. A., Ruhm, C., & Waldfogel, J. (2004). *Does pre-kindergarten improve school preparation and performance?* NBER Working Paper No. W10452.

McCartney, K., & Weiss, H. (2006). Data in a democracy: the evolving role of evaluation in policy and program development. In J. L. Aber, S. J. Bishop-Josef, S. M. Jones, K. T. McLearn & D. A. Phillips (Eds.), *Child development and social policy: Knowledge for action* (59–76). Washington, DC: American Psychological Association.

Newcombe, N. S. (2003). Some controls control too much. *Child Development*, **74**, 1050–1052.

NICHD Early Child Care Research Network. (2005). *Child care and child development: Results from the NICHD study of early child care and youth development*. New York: Guilford Press.

NICHD Early Child Care Research Network.Duncan, G. J. (2003). Modeling the impacts of child care quality on children's preschool cognitive development. *Child Development*, **74**, 1454–1475.

Pitts, S. C., Prost, J. H., & Winters, J. J. (2004). Quasi-experimental designs in developmental research: Design and analysis considerations. In D. M. Teti (Ed.), *Handbook of research methods in developmental science*. Malden, MA: Blackwell Publishing.

Rivkin, S. G., Hanushek, E. A., & Kain, J. F. (2005). Teachers, schools, and academic achievement. *Econometrica*, **73**, 417–458.

Rosenbaum, P. R., & Rubin, D. B. (1983). The central role of the propensity score in observational studies for causal effects. *Biometrika*, **70**, 41–55.

Rubin, D. B. (1978). Bayesian inference for causal effects: The role of randomization. *Annals of Statistics*, **6**, 34–58.

Rubin, D. B. (1997). Estimating causal effects from large datasets using propensity scores. *Annals of Internal Medicine*, **127**, 757–763.

Rubinfeld, D. L. (2000). Reference guide on multiple regression, in *Federal Judicial Center, Reference Manual on Scientific Evidence*, 2nd ed., pp.179–227. (available at http://www.fjc.gov/public/pdf.nsf/lookup/11.mult_reg.pdf/$File/11.mult_reg.pdf).

Shadish, W. R., Cook, T. D., & Campbell, D. T. (2002). *Experimental and quasi-experimental designs for generalized causal inference*. Boston: Houghton-Mifflin.

Tabachnick, B. G., & Fidell, L. S. (1996). *Using multivariate statistics* (3rd ed.). New York: Harper Collins Publishers.

Thistlewaite, D., & Campbell, D. (1960). Regression-discontinuity analysis: An alternative to the ex-post facto experiment. *Journal of Educational Psychology*, **51**, 309–317.

Winship, C., & Morgan, S. L. (1999). The estimation of causal effects from observational data. *Annual Review of Sociology*, **25**, 659–706.

VII. THE PRACTICAL IMPORTANCE OF FINDINGS

We can think of them as building blocks, the research reports that populate our journals. They are what we train our students to make; as they accumulate we use them to build solid edifices of understanding, at least, that is our hope. In this chapter I offer suggestions about materials to employ and ways to shape these individual blocks so that they do not disappear into an unread archive, but instead stand out, able and ready to become part of those structures of accumulated understanding we hope to build. I emphasize what is sometimes, literally, an overlooked part of an article, the results section. To change metaphors, this is the part students and colleagues occasionally confess to skipping on their way from the appetizer introduction to the desert discussion; it seems somehow expendable. This seems risky, even foolhardy, because it is here, in the results section, that the practical importance of findings is more likely revealed. By practical importance of findings I do not mean how to make babies into geniuses or how to protect them from scrapes with the law. Instead I mean, no matter the substantive content of an empirical study, how to reveal its findings in ways that are clear and fairly represent what our data tell us about the phenomena at hand. I tend to think of the numbers collected during the course of a study as forming an uncarved block. It is our job as data analysts to sculpt the block until the story embedded in it can be released and seen clearly. As you might guess from these comments, the emphasis of this chapter will be much more on description than statistical inference, on the size of effects than statistical significance.

Here is the plan. In the course of this chapter I consider three topics, not exhaustively but in ways that illustrate some guidelines for practices that help reveal the practical importance of findings. A graphical thread runs throughout. First, I emphasize the importance of data screening using graphical methods and illustrate with Tukey's (1977) box-and-whisker plot. Second, I suggest that when presenting results there is merit in keeping analysis and description separate and illustrate by reviewing suggestions that error bars be used for analysis. Third—and this is central—along with many others I describe the pernicious effects of excessive reliance on statistical significance testing, recommend presentation and interpretation of effect sizes as the appropriate cure, and illustrate with partial eta squared (symbolized $p\eta^2$) and the odds ratio. Most of this is not new; a particularly cogent summary of problems and a useful list of references was offered a few years ago by Wilkinson and the Task Force on Statistical Inference (1999), which I cite several times in the course of this chapter.

Much of what I write here is based on a general principle, adapted from Edward Tufte's wonderful *The Visual Display of Quantitative Information* (1983). Tufte writes of the data–ink ratio and recommends that it be large. Use only as much ink—in a figure, in a table, in prose—as needed to convey the data clearly; more is unnecessary and unnecessarily distracting. Thus, for example, the three-dimensional bars, produced too easily by Excel and seen in too may PowerPoint presentations, diminish the data–ink ratio, clutter the screen or page, provide no useful information, and should be avoided (Tufte calls them chart-junk).

DATA SCREENING: DISTRIBUTIONS, OUTLIERS, AND VARIABILITY

Data in hand, eager investigators often rush to analysis (correlations, analyses of variance, etc.), but two steps come first: data screening and univariate description. Data screening can seem unglamorous but is essential; undetected data anomalies cloud analysis and undermine accurate interpretation, which makes the discovery of the practical importance of findings difficult to impossible at the outset. Before all else, look at your data; use graphical methods that show all data points (Wilkinson et al., 1999) or at least summaries that are more revealing than just a mean and standard deviation. Examine how data are distributed (Tabachnick & Fidell, 2007); for example, if 40–50% of the scores for a given variable are 0, perhaps that variable should be recoded as binary (0 or 1) and not analyzed as though it were a reasonably distributed continuous variable.

Outliers should also be identified: Are they data entry errors, extreme but informative cases, or indicative of cases that should be excluded from the sample? How are they defined? One common definition is worth re-examining, first because it may increase our skepticism concerning received wisdom, and second because it motivates us to consider variability and how it is portrayed generally. Outliers are often defined as any data point greater than three standard deviations (*SD*) from the mean. However, all data points, including putative outliers, are used to compute both mean and *SD*, and outliers influence their values considerably. Consider the three almost identical sets of 20 scores shown in Figure 1. Most scores pile up around 500

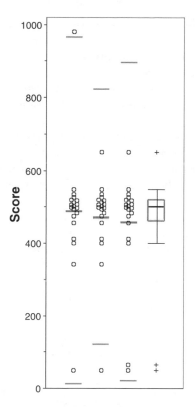

FIGURE 1.—Three sets of 20 scores each that differ by two scores at most; each score is indicated with a circle. For each set, the thicker horizontal line in the center indicates the mean; thinner horizontal lines, top and bottom, indicate plus and minus three standard deviations from the mean. The box-and-whisker plot at the right is for the set of scores immediately to its left; extreme scores (see text for definition) are indicated with plus signs.

but the leftmost set has one extremely high and one extremely low score. A few more low scores pull the mean down to 488 (thicker horizontal line at center) and the extreme scores result in a large standard deviation (159; thinner horizontal lines, top and bottom, indicate three SDs from the mean); only the extremely high score is an outlier by the usual three-SD criterion. If the highest score moved toward the mean (the middle set), thereby decreasing both mean (472) and SD (117), only the lowest score would be an outlier. And if the second lowest score moved toward 0 (the rightmost set), thereby decreasing the mean (458) but increasing the SD (146), no scores would be outliers. This demonstration should lead us to look at graphical displays of raw data more and rely on purely mechanical definitions (e.g., > 3 SDs makes it an outlier) less.

The master of data description is John Tukey, whose *Exploratory Data Analysis* (1977) deserves to be widely read. In particular, his box-and-whisker plots suggest a way to identify outliers that is less vulnerable to the vagaries of a few extreme scores. They also provide information about variables that is far more informative than the means and standard deviations typically provided. The box defines the range within which half the scores fall: Its top is the 75th percentile, its bottom the 25th, and a horizontal line in the middle defines the median (50th percentile), thus the height of the box is the interquartile range (IQR). Extreme scores (i.e., potential outliers) are defined as any scores that are $1\frac{1}{2}$ times the IQR above the top or below the bottom of the box (although another factor such as two or three could be used). Whiskers extend from the lowest to the highest scores not defined as extreme and extreme scores are indicated with a mark beyond the whisker (see Figure 1). Thus the box-and-whisker approach defines extreme scores similarly for all three data sets in Figure 1 (the highest and two lowest; the plot indicates extreme scores for the rightmost of the three sets with plus signs). Moreover, the box-and-whisker plot portrays how these scores are distributed in a way that the mean and *SD* alone do not: the greater proportion in the box below the median and the longer lower whisker reveal a negative skew.

In sum, at its best initial data screening considers graphic portrayal of all data points, such as the three distributions shown at the left of Figure 1, although summary graphic devices, such as the box-and-whisker plot shown at the right of Figure 1, are also useful. Box-and-whisker plots are also useful when presenting results, as demonstrated in the next section.

PRESENTING RESULTS: ANALYSIS AND ERROR BARS

A typical study usually includes a number of variables, perhaps dozens but at least a handful. As noted earlier, the first step is to examine scores for each variable so that anomalies can be addressed before analysis begins. The second step includes univariate description of those variables, which is how most results sections begin. Here I want to focus on a third step, the presentation of results as guided by the analyses performed. In the process I consider recent suggestions for presenting analytic results in figures using error bars and suggest that, at least given the current stage in development, there is merit in presenting analytic results and descriptive data separately, and not asking error bars to do double duty. I illustrate these points with a worked example and discuss merits of different sorts of descriptive figures. My assumption is that understanding the practical importance of findings begins with clear and accurate description.

As an example, I use data from Lauren Adamson and her colleagues (e.g., Adamson, Bakeman, & Deckner, 2004). When observing mothers with their toddlers in a structured situation, we define four ways they can be jointly engaged, which we term states of nonsymbol-infused (NSI) supported, NSI coordinated, symbol-infused (SI) supported, and SI coordinated engagement. In recent work (Adamson, Deckner, & Bakeman, 2006), we compared these four types of joint engagement states in three groups of 30-month-olds (55 typically developing children, eight verbal children with autism, and 11 nonverbal children with autism). This design suggests a two-factor (3×4), mixed-design analysis of variance with three groups between subjects and the four engagement state scores as repeated measures, which is a kind of design often encountered in our literature. A main effect for group would indicate that the groups differed in their mean amounts of joint engagement, a main effect for type of state would indicate that some types were more common than others, whereas a significant interaction would mean the states varied differently by group.

For these data all three effects were significant at the .001 level; the effect size ($p\eta^2$) for group was .55, for state again .55, and for their interaction .40. Because the interaction is significant, it makes sense to present means broken down by both group and state; thus a table with the 12 subgroup means given in Table 1 would result. Now we have a choice. The significant interaction indicates moderation (see Dearing & Hamilton, this volume), but depending on how we conceptualize matters, either group or state (but not both) could be designated as the moderator. If we wanted to

TABLE 1

TYPICAL MEAN AND STANDARD DEVIATION TABLE AUGMENTED WITH EFFECT-SIZE STATISTICS AND POST HOC RESULTS

Joint Engagement State	Group			Statistic	
	Nonverbal Autistic	Verbal Autistic	Typical	$p\eta^2$	p
NSI Supported	41_a (11)	34_a (11)	22_b (11)	.32	<.001
SI Supported	2_a (2)	20_b (8)	34_c (12)	.54	<.001
NSI Coordinated	2 (2)	4 (2)	5 (4)	.07	.083
SI Coordinated	1_a (1)	5_a (5)	15_b (10)	.29	<.001

Note.—Scores are mean percentages; $n = 11, 8$, and 55 for the nonverbal autistic, verbal autistic, and typical groups, respectively (*SD*s are in parentheses); see text for source. Means for each variable that do not differ significantly per a Tukey's post hoc test, $p < .05$, share a common subscript. Partial eta squares indicate the size of the group effect for each variable.

131

emphasize how individual states differed by group (i.e., treat group as the moderator), we might follow-up the significant interaction with simple analyses of group effects for each state separately. The effects sizes for these analyses, along with results of Tukey's post hoc tests when these were significant, could then be added to Table 1, as shown here. In general, Table 1 has a form I would recommend: not only are means displayed, broken down as suggested by the analysis, but effect sizes—in this case, for the follow-up analyses—are also displayed along with post hoc test results that indicate exactly how the displayed means vary.

Often analyses such as the one just presented are supplemented with a figure like Figure 2, here organized by group then state to emphasize how state profiles varied among the groups. Such bar graphs—the height of a bar indicates a particular mean value—has the merit of making the relative sizes of the means visible in a way Table 1 does not. Occasionally journal editors, remembering the days when figures added to printing costs, may object to the apparent redundancy of Table 1 and Figure 2, but including them both has real merit. First, as Wilkinson et al. (1999) noted, it helps to provide both tables and figures because individuals have different preferences for processing complex information. Second, this table and figure are only partially redundant. Including the figure, which presents information about variability (the error bars) could let us eliminate the four rows of *SD*s from the table, thereby removing clutter, making the table easier to read, and improving the combined table-and-figure data–ink ratio. Moreover, the table contains information about effect size and statistical significance that

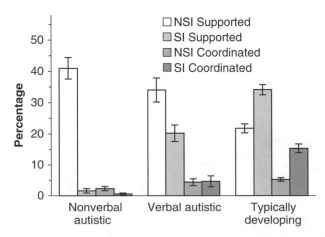

FIGURE 2.—A typical figure showing means and standard errors. Mean percentages for nonsymbol-infused (NSI) supported, symbol-infused (SI) supported, NSI coordinated, and SI coordinated joint engagement for nonverbal autistic, verbal autistic, and typical groups ($n = 11$, 8, and 55, respectively) are shown; for source, see text. Error bars represent standard errors of the mean.

the figure does not. Figure 2, which adds error bars to the usual mean bars, can be regarded as an improvement over the unadorned bar graphs often seen; the error bars remind us that the mean bars indicate not true values but sample means, which are subject to sampling error. Still, there are many kinds of error bars, and the figure caption should identify the kind, especially as researchers may confuse them (Bella, Fidler, Williams, & Cumming, 2005); for example, Figure 2 portrays standard errors of the mean (SEM). These are probably the most common kind and the kind most likely used when error bars are otherwise unidentified, but error bars could represent 95% confidence intervals (CIs), which has the effect of approximately doubling the length of the error bar (or more than doubling when samples are extremely small).

Each error bar like those in Figure 2 indicates variability for a single mean, which is why the lengths vary; the n data points used to compute each mean are also used to compute its SD and SEM (SD divided by square root of n). Computation is easy but interpretation is more complex. Consider a 95% CI, which computationally is the SEM multiplied by the .05 critical value of t for $n-1$ degrees of freedom. It is not correct to say that there is a 95% probability that the population mean falls within the interval (Cumming & Finch, 2005); better to say that if we conducted similar studies countless times, 95% of the time the population mean would fall within the interval specified because this takes into account that a mean computed for the single study at hand could, due to sampling, deviate considerably from its population value. At first glance the 95% CI, which appears to bridge description and inference, might seem preferable to the usual SEM error bar, which is more purely a descriptive device (albeit one that combines information about variability with sample size). After all, if a 95% CI does not include 0, we can infer that its mean differs significantly from 0, $p < .05$. Might CIs then be used to portray more complex analytic results directly? For example, could we not use CIs to determine directly which bars in Figure 2 differ significantly from others without referring to the post hoc results provided in Table 1? A series of articles has been devoted to this enterprise (e.g., Cumming & Finch, 2005; Loftus, 1993; Fidler & Thompson, 2001; Masson & Loftus, 2003), but matters quickly become complex, which is especially true for designs that include repeated measures (Bakeman & McArthur, 1996; Loftus & Masson, 1994). For one thing, description is compromised; to portray analytic results, error bars need to be based on mean squares for error, which apply to the group of scores as defined by the effect analyzed, with the result that groups of error bars would have the same length even when the SDs associated with individual means varied.

CIs have their partisans, among them Fidler, Thomason, Cumming, Finch, and Leeman (2004), who noted that, even when editors insisted that articles include CIs, authors who presented them often failed to use them as a basis for inference. In response, Rouder and Morey (2005) suggested this may not be such a bad thing, and recommended that a-relational CIs, the kind usually encountered drawn around a single sample or subsample mean, (as in Figure 2), be distinguished from relational CIs, ones that represent group or condition difference and whose "most salient disadvantage is the lack of standard conventions for constructing and describing those intervals" (p. 77). Rouder and Morey noted that a-relational CIs are useful because they provide a rough guide to the variability in the data and a quick check for the heterogeneity of variance. They recommended that a-relational CIs be coupled with statistical tests, which provide more precise information about comparisons; Table 1 and Figure 2 taken together can be viewed as an illustration of their advice.

The exchange Fidler et al. (2004) initiated strikes me as useful, although my conclusion differs some from theirs. In response to Rouder and Morey (2005), Fidler, Thomason, Cumming, Finch, and Leeman (2005) argued that representation of variability in the data and checks on heterogeneity of variance should be based on the SD not a CI, on a descriptive not an inferential statistic. I agree with Fidler et al. (2005) that Rouder and Morey's comments in fact reinforce the need to report standard deviations—although I might say, variance generally. Thus I conclude that replacing figures like Figure 2, which portray a-relational CIs, with figures that portray variability descriptively, which box-and-whisker plots do admirably, has real merit and is a strategy worthy of serious consideration.

In sum, given the current state of the literature (e.g., Blouin & Riopelle, 2005), it makes sense to present analytic and descriptive results separately, as Rouder and Morey (2005) suggested; even Fidler et al. (2005) concluded that "What to construct CIs around—and how to display them—remain issues for debate" (p. 405). When describing how means differ, I am not convinced that unadorned bar graphs (Figure 2 without the error bars) are very useful; they require little ink but present few data so the data–ink ratio is not especially favorable. Bar graphs adorned with error bars, like Figure 2, are an improvement (and are frequently encountered), but more informative alternatives might be welcome. Fidler et al. (2005) suggested that SDs might better convey variability than CIs, but SDs also reflect sample size, which can be a disadvantage when groups vary considerably in size, as in Figure 2. For a more informative alternative to both SDs and CIs, we need only return to the previous section, and consider box-and-whisker plots (see Figure 3).

Figures 2 and 3 are based on the same raw data; Figure 3 uses a bit more ink but conveys considerably more information, thus it represents an improvement in the data–ink ratio. Figure 2 provides only means and indications of variability, although the unequal sample sizes compromise comparability. In contrast, Figure 3 provides the same information as

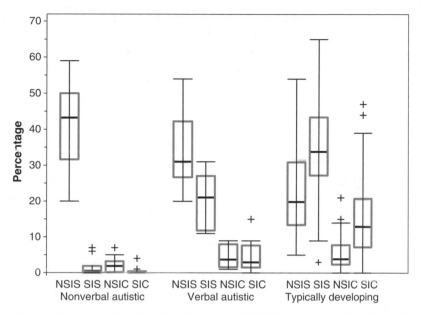

FIGURE 3.—Box-and-whisker plots for nonsymbol-infused supported (NSIS), symbol-infused supported (SIS), nonsymbol-infused coordinated (NSIC), and symbol-infused coordinated (SIC) joint engagement; $n = 11$, 8, and 55 for the nonverbal autistic, verbal autistic, and typically developing groups, respectively.

Figure 2, and considerably more. Consider the sorts of conclusions Figure 3 affords. (A) For nonverbal autistic children, the NSI supported state predominated. Specifically about 75% of the NSI-supported scores were above 30%. Conversely, about 75% of NSI-supported scores for typically developing children were below 30%. Moreover, for the nonverbal autistic children, about 50%, 25%, and 75% of their SI supported, NSI coordinated, and SI coordinated scores, respectively, were 0 (the middle, bottom, and top of these boxes is about 0), which is important descriptive information often lost in the usual mean-and-SD table or bar graph figure. (B) For verbal autistic children, the supported state predominated. Essentially all supported scores (both NSI and SI) were higher than all coordinated scores (both NSI and SI). (C) For typically developing children, scores were higher for supported states generally but with considerable variability. Finally, at least 75% of these children had higher SI coordinated scores than any of the children with autism. The statistical analysis informed us that the profiles varied by group, but Figure 3 shows us exactly how in a way that provides more information even than post hoc tests on means and certainly more information than the conventional Figure 2.

As investigators see the merit and the need, it seems likely that software developers will provide programs that produce figures like Figure 3 more automatically. After all, in earlier versions, Excel could not put error bars on bar graphs as it does now, and SPSS already provides a way to display box-and-whisker plots for several groups on one axis. Programs for box-and-whisker plots that provide more control over labels, fonts, and other stylistic elements, thereby producing better-quality figures for publication, cannot be far away and would encourage more routine use of these helpful plots.

THE SIZE OF EFFECTS AND THE END OF SIGNIFICANCE

Clear, concrete description of results, as illustrated in the previous section, is one foundational stepping stone to revealing the practical importance of findings. Another is an intense focus on the size of the effects described. Increasingly, those who reflect on research practice have come to view a narrow focus on the statistical significance of findings, a focus that has dominated much of our thinking about data analysis for more than half a century, as something of a will-o'-the-wisp, beckoning us further into the swamp of false certainty (e.g., Cohen, 1990, 1994; Rosnow & Rosenthal, 1989; Wilkinson et al., 1999).

The traditional landscape of statistical inference has been dominated by the .05 cliff and a fear of saying things that are not so. Most of us were taught to set our alpha level at the conventional .05, thereby ensuring that the probability of making a false claim (a Type I error) would be .05. Not emphasized was the conditional nature of this statement; the probability is .05 if and only if there genuinely is no effect. As Cohen pungently reminded us (1990), if something is so, claiming an effect is never false; when there is an effect, however small, the probably of a Type I error is 0; and "So if the null hypothesis is always false, what's the big deal about rejecting it?" (p. 1308).

The big deal is, too many of us—researchers, reviewers, and journal editors alike—appear to have embraced the false belief that if a result is not statistically significant, then there is no effect; any apparent effect is just chance. If a result is significant, $p < .05$, we can discuss it; if not, and we mention it, journal editors may slap our hands. It is as though Cohen (1990) never wrote, ".05 is not a cliff but a convenient reference point along the possibility—probability continuum" (p. 1311), or as Rosnow and Rosenthal (1989) quipped, "surely, God loves the .06 nearly as much as the .05" (p. 1277). The all-or-nothing approach—statistical significance indicates an effect but insignificance indicates no effect—permeates especially introductions to empirical reports, which too often inform us that A affects B but does not affect C, and base such all-or-nothing statements on whether or not statistical significance was reported in previous literature. However, statistical significance should not overly impress us. After all, even the most

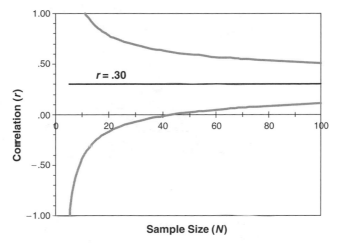

FIGURE 4.—95% confidence intervals (curved lines, top and bottom) for a correlation (r) of .30 (horizontal line), given different sample sizes (N). When N is 44 or greater, the confidence intervals do not include 0, indicating a statistically significant correlation, $p < .05$.

miniscule effect can achieve statistical significance if the sample size is large enough. Consider Figure 4. The curved lines, top and bottom, demarcate the 95% CIs for a correlation coefficient of .30 (horizontal line); thus, the figure shows how the interval decreases as sample size increases. The x-axis is crossed when $N = 44$, which signals the transition from insignificance into glorious statistical significance, $p < .05$—although the magnitude of the effect, $r = .30$, remains unchanged. A similar figure could be made for $r = .10$, usually regarded as a weak correlation, which becomes statistically significant, $p < .05$, when $N = 385$. Incidentally, Figure 4 illustrates a use of 95% CIs recommended by Wilkinson et al. (1999), not for sets of group means as in Figure 2, but for an effect size involving one of a study's principle outcomes. When CIs for an effect (here, a simple correlation) almost but not quite include 0, the effect is revealed as weak; the further 0 lies outside the CIs, the stronger the effect.

When statistical significance is emphasized and the size of effects is deemphasized or ignored, which characterizes most research reports for the last several decades, our literature suffers (Schmidt, 1996). Consider Figure 5, which introduces a second common effect–size statistic, Cohen's d, defined as the standardized difference between the means of two groups we wish to compare (see Table 2 for descriptions of this and other effect–size statistics mentioned in this chapter). For the Figure 5 example, which is based on one given by Schmidt, the null hypothesis is that the means are not different, so per the null hypothesis d would equal 0. Assume that both groups include 15 cases ($N = 30$). Then the standard error of d would be .38

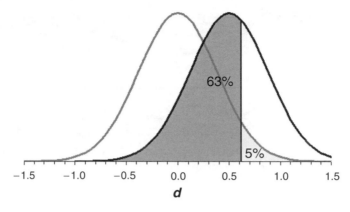

63%

5%

−1.5 −1.0 −0.5 0.0 0.5 1.0 1.5

d

FIGURE 5.—Sampling distributions for Cohen's d, the standardized difference between two group means, for the null hypothesis world, for which $d = 0$, and for the real world, for which $d = .5$. When $N = 30$ and $d = .62$ or greater, the null hypothesis is rejected (light gray area labeled 5%); however the probability of a missed effect (a Type II error) is 63%, (the dark gray area).

(i.e., the square root of $1/14 + 1/14$) and its one-tailed .05 critical value, derived from the unit-normal distribution, would be .62 ($.38 \times 1.645$).

The normal curve centered on $d = 0$ in Figure 5 represents the fictitious null hypothesis world, that is, the sampling distribution for d if the null hypothesis were true; the light gray area labeled 5% indicates values that, per usual null-hypothesis testing conventions, allow us to reject the null. However, assume we know that in fact $d = .5$, an effect size Cohen characterized as medium (Cohen, 1988). Thus the normal curve centered on $d = .5$ represents the "real world" and indicates the real sampling distribution for d. The probability of making a false claim (a Type I error) is 0, as noted earlier, but the probability of missing a real effect (a Type II error) is a sobering .63; if d did not exceed the critical value of .62 but instead fell in the range indicated by the darker gray area we would not reject the null hypothesis.

If diligent investigators performed study after study with $N = 30$, they would report statistically significant results only 37% of the time (worse, for a t and not a z test as here, power is .35, and for a two-tailed t test, power is .26). To be significant ($d > .62$) an effect must be 24% larger than the true effect ($d = .50$). Significant effects would average .89, which is 78% larger than the true effect. As 63% of the studies would find no effect, the conclusion would be that none exists. However, as 37% of the studies would find a large effect, the conclusion would be that further research is needed to identify the moderator variable(s) responsible. Thus undue reliance on null-hypothesis significance testing can actually impede our discovering features of the real world, in this case that there is a straightforward but moderate effect (Schmidt, 1996).

138

TABLE 2
ILLUSTRATIVE EFFECT-SIZE STATISTICS

Statistic	Definition	Comment
d	$\dfrac{M_1 - M_2}{SE_D}$	Cohen's d, the standardized difference between two sample means. Widely used whenever two groups are compared. Commonly used in formal meta-analytic studies. Computations for SS_D, the standard error of the mean difference, vary (see e.g., Rosenthal, 1994).
r	$\dfrac{\sum z_X z_Y}{N}$	Pearson's product moment correlation. Perhaps the most widely used index in psychology of the degree of association between two (usually continuous) variables. Commonly used in formal meta-analytic studies. One definition is, the average cross-product of the z scores; it is also the square root of R^2 appropriately signed.
ΔR^2	$\dfrac{SS_{\text{change}}}{SS_{\text{total}}}$	Change in proportion of variance accounted for when an additional variable(s) is added in a hierarchic regression step. An intuitively understood measure of the predictive power (effect) of a variable or set of variables; useful when comparing the magnitude of different effects within and across studies.
$p\eta^2$	$\dfrac{SS_{\text{effect}}}{SS_{\text{effect}} + SS_{\text{error}}}$	Partial eta squared; the proportion of error plus effect variance accounted for by an effect (same as ΔR^2 for one-way ANOVA designs); used primarily when describing analysis of variance results. Useful when comparing the magnitude of different effects within and across studies.
OR	$\dfrac{x_{11}/x_{12}}{x_{21}/x_{22}}$	Odds ratio (x_{ij} represents the cells of a 2×2 table); literally, the odds of a particular (binary) outcome given circumstance A divided by the odds of the outcome given circumstance B. Widely used in epidemiology, less so in psychology, perhaps because binary outcomes are more frequent in epidemiology. Commonly used in formal meta-analytic studies.

The antidote, which is increasingly appreciated but still not sufficiently practiced, is provided by what I earlier called an intense focus on effect sizes. The advantages are overwhelming (Wilkinson et al., 1999). When effect sizes occupy center stage in results sections, accumulating patterns of results across studies are more evident—and more likely to provide the needed grist for a subsequent meta-analyst's mill. The dark influence of the under discussed variable of sample size, which leads us to regard as real a correlation of .30 only when the sample size is 44 or more, is minimized, as are other distorting influences on our literature (Schmidt, 1996). Further, when effect sizes are emphasized, we are more likely to confront issues of real-world importance, and perhaps in the process argue that in some areas of research seemingly small effect sizes can have important practical consequences (McCartney & Rosenthal, 2000), which can only deepen understanding the practical importance of our findings. Why are effect sizes not more emphasized, given their advantages? McCartney and Rosenthal

(2000) suggested two reasons: knowledge and sense. Investigators may lack the knowledge required to compute and report estimates of effect sizes and, beyond knowledge, may lack an intuitive sense of how to interpret the magnitude of effects once computed. Knowledge is more easily remedied. Excellent summaries of common effect sizes are easy to find: two of the most common and simplest have already appeared in this chapter (r and d) and McCartney and Rosenthal, among many others (see e.g., the volume edited by Cooper & Hedges, 1994), provide excellent summaries and useful comments.

Choice of which effect sizes to present is partly convention, partly taste. McCartney and Rosenthal (2000), for example, emphasize the r family (bivariate association) and the d family (comparison of two means)—partly because of their utility in meta-analyses—and de-emphasize squared indexes such as the change in R^2 of hierarchic multiple regression and the conceptually similar $p\eta^2$ of analyses of variance (see Tables 1 and 2). However, others may find squared indexes intuitively appealing, especially for descriptive purposes: while the meaning of the magnitude of r seems elusive—Is .6 compared with .5 as much more correlation as .3 compared with .2?—a statement such as gender accounts for 23% of the variation in self-esteem scores seems informative and readily understood. For those using analyses of variance, $p\eta^2$ has another advantage; its values are provided by standard statistical programs such as SPSS and, in any case, easily computed from F-ratios:

$$p\eta^2 = \frac{SS_{\text{effect}}}{SS_{\text{effect}} + SS_{\text{error}}} = \frac{F \times df_{\text{effect}}}{F \times df_{\text{effect}} + df_{\text{error}}}$$

(the formula with SS is definitional, the one with F is derived from it algebraically), thus authors can compare their effect sizes with ones from other studies, as long as the other studies included F-ratios, as is typical. One caveat: any variables compared with partial η^2 should be all between-subjects or all within-subjects; when comparing effects for a variable that is between-subjects in some studies and within-subjects in others (e.g., age), use generalized η^2 instead (Bakeman, 2005; Olejnik & Algina, 2003).

Another effect size statistic, useful for binary data but underutilized by psychologists, is worth presenting. The odds ratio is easy to compute and admits to simple and concrete interpretation. Consider this example. Deborah Deckner (Deckner, Adamson, & Bakeman, 2003) wanted to know whether mothers and their toddlers matched each other's rhythmic vocalizations and so coded onset and offset times for mothers' and toddlers' rhythmic vocalizations. Table 3 shows results for one dyad and considers whether toddlers matched mothers. For the rows, seconds were classified as within (or not) a 5-second window defined by when the mother began a

TABLE 3

ODDS RATIO EXAMPLE: EFFECT OF MOTHER'S RHYTHMIC VOCALIZATIONS ON ONSET OF
TODDLER'S RHYTHMIC VOCALIZATIONS

	Toddler Onset		
Within 5 Seconds of Mother's Onset	Yes	No	Totals
Yes	11	189	200
No	29	971	1,000
Totals	40	1,160	1,200

Note.—The tallying unit is a second; the table cross-classifies seconds by whether or not they occurred within 5 seconds of an onset of mother rhythmic vocalization and by whether or not an onset of a toddler rhythmic vocalization occurred. This mother–toddler dyad was observed for 20 minutes, so 1,200 seconds. For these data, the odds ratio is 1.95; see text.

rhythmic vocalization, whereas columns indicated whether or not the toddler began a rhythmic vocalization during that second.

For this example, the odds that the toddler began a rhythmic vocalization shortly after his mother did were 11–189 (i.e., .0582–1 or 1–17.2), whereas the corresponding odds otherwise were 29–971 (i.e., .0299–1 or 1–33.5); thus, the odds ratio was 1.95 (i.e., .0582/.0299 or [11/189] ÷ [29/971]). The concrete interpretation is, this toddler was about twice as likely to begin a rhythmic vocalization shortly after his mother did than at other times; he tended to match. More generally, an odds ratio lets us make statements of the general form, behavior C as opposed to not-C is N times more likely (or less, if the odds ratio is less than one) given behavior R as opposed to not-R. For example, rows could represent treatment versus not and columns staying healthy versus getting sick; then the odds ratio would indicate how much greater (or less) the chance of staying healthy was, given treatment compared with no treatment. Assuming appropriate binary data, such statements are easily understood, convey the importance of an effect directly, and deserve to be more widely used. Moreover, the odds ratio is standard in fields such as epidemiology and is similar in spirit to the binomial effect size display or BESD proposed by Rosenthal and Rubin (1982) for r.

Greater knowledge of effect size statistics is the easy part. Even if editors required and investigators complied, so that estimates of effect sizes were routinely presented in published articles, this would not guarantee that what McCartney and Rosenthal (2000) called sense would grow apace. We can image a future article, similar to Fidler et al. (2004), but with a slightly modified title: "Editors can lead researchers to effect sizes, but can't make them think." The hard part remains developing intuitive feelings for the practical importance of whatever are the most appropriate effect sizes in various areas of research. Among other notions, we need to shed the idea that smaller numbers are not meaningful, which I suspect accounts in large part for why investigators often prefer to emphasize statistics like r and not r^2. One caveat however: this does not mean that small Ns are universally fine; larger sample sizes give us more confidence in the accuracy of the effect sizes we report.

Primarily, an intense focus on effect sizes throughout our research reports is needed, not just in the results section (even though this alone could aid future meta-analysts) but in the introduction and discussion as well. Meaningful consideration of effect magnitudes in introductions that avoided the all-or-nothing quality mentioned earlier would be especially welcome. Such introductions need not be mini meta-analyses, but incorporating a meta-analytical way of thinking when citing previous literature, considering size and not just presence–absence of effects, would help us develop interpretive sense in specific research areas and be in a position to present more convincingly the practical importance of our findings.

Much of the literature cited here reveals a deep dis-ease with null hypothesis significance tests (NHSTs) as practiced by our field for the last half-century or so. In a recent article, Killeen (2005a) has suggested an alternative to NHSTs. The APA (2000) recommends reporting the exact probability value obtained from the statistical test, that is, the probability of obtaining a result as extreme or more extreme than the one actually obtained if the null hypothesis is in fact true (call it p_{test}). Killeen recommends reporting instead the probability of replication (p_{rep}), defined as the likelihood that future studies would find "an effect of the same sign as that found in the original experiment" (p. 346). The advantage is, unlike "the triple-negative no-man's land of failure to reject the null" (p. 349), p_{rep} is a positive statement about results. The disadvantage is, like p_{test}, p_{rep} is an estimate; both are affected in similar ways by sample size and both can mislead when the original study is a "victim" of sampling error (Cumming, 2005; Killeen, 2005b), which occurs when, due to the bad luck of the draw, the original results do not reflect reality well. It is too early to tell whether p_{rep} will be embraced (for concerns, see Macdonald, 2005; for a response, see Killeen, 2005b); more narrowly, Killeen's argument shows that the magnitude of both p_{test} and p_{rep} convey important information (contradicting those generations of instructors who told us not to refer to one effect as "more significant" than another). No matter whether p_{test} or p_{rep} is reported, and no matter whether standard parametric or randomization tests (see, last paragraph, Killeen, 2005b) are performed, the magnitude of effect sizes, as discussed in the paragraphs before this one, remain crucial to understanding the importance of our findings. Although it is not yet clear whether Killeen's p_{rep} will become widely adopted as an alternative to p_{test}, his article convinced me anew of the importance of discussion that focuses on the magnitude of the effects we find.

CONCLUSION

In this chapter, I have made three types of suggestions, all designed to increase the chances that we and others will better comprehend the practical importance of our findings. To return to the building block analogy, good blocks need to be made of sturdy stuff, which I have equated with careful attention paid to initial data screening, an enterprise greatly aided by graphical methods. Then, when it comes to shaping our sturdy blocks, presenting our results, I have suggested that analytical results be explicated with figures that remain faithful to the data, uncompromised by inferential information better conveyed in tables and prose. Moreover, "Figures attract the reader's eye and help convey global results. . . . It is time for authors to take advantage of them and for editors and reviewers to urge authors to do so" (Wilkinson et al., 1999, p. 601). Finally, what I characterized earlier as an intense focus on effect sizes is the mortar, the stuff that holds blocks together and lets us build what I earlier called edifices of understanding. The advice given in the current Publication Manual is a start: "For the reader to fully understand the importance of your findings, it is almost always necessary to include some index of effect size or strength of relationship in your Results section" (American Psychological Association [APA], 2000, p. 25). Beyond such reporting, which at least facilitates future meta-analyses, effect-size thinking needs to permeate introduction and discussion sections as well. Maybe this is the roof our edifice needs: vigorous discussion followed, we hope, by emerging consensus and convincing rationales for specific magnitudes that, for specific domains and specific variables, are practically important.

ACKNOWLEDGMENT

Thanks to my colleagues Deborah F. Deckner and Christopher Henrich, and students Raymond Becker and Leanne Valentine, who provided helpful comments on an earlier draft.

REFERENCES

Adamson, L. B., Bakeman, R., & Deckner, D. (2004). The development of symbol-infused joint engagement. *Child Development*, **75**, 1171–1187.

Adamson, L. B., Deckner, D., & Bakeman, R. (2006). *Symbol-infused joint engagement in young children with autism.* Unpublished manuscript.

American Psychological Association. (2000). *Publication manual of the American Psychological Association* (5th ed.). Washington, DC: Author.

143

Bakeman, R. (2005). Recommended effect size statistics for repeated measures designs. *Behavior Research Methods*, **37**, 379–384.

Bakeman, R., & McArthur, D. (1996). Picturing repeated measures: Comments on Loftus, Morrison, and others. *Behavior Research Methods, Instruments, and Computers*, **28**, 584–589.

Bella, S., Fidler, F., Williams, J., & Cumming, G. (2005). Researchers misunderstand confidence intervals and standard error bars. *Psychological Methods*, **10**, 389–396.

Blouin, D. C., & Riopelle, A. J. (2005). On confidence intervals for within-subjects designs. *Psychological Methods*, **10**, 397–412.

Cohen, J. (1988). *Statistical power analysis for the behavioral sciences* (2nd ed.). Hillsdale, NJ: Erlbaum.

Cohen, J. (1990). Things I have learned (so far). *American Psychologist*, **45**, 1304–1312.

Cohen, J. (1994). The earth is round ($p < .05$). *American Psychologist*, **49**, 997–1003.

Cooper, H., & Hedges, L. V. (1994). *The handbook of research synthesis*. New York: Russell Sage Foundation.

Cumming, G. (2005). Understanding the average probability of replication: Comment on Killeen (2005). *Psychological Science*, **16**, 1002–1004.

Cumming, G., & Finch, S. (2005). Inference by eye: Confidence intervals and how to read pictures of data. *American Psychologist*, **60**, 170–180.

Deckner, D. F., Adamson, L. B., & Bakeman, R. (2003). Rhythm in mother–infant interactions. *Infancy*, **4**, 201–217.

Fidler, F., & Thompson, B. (2001). Computing correct confidence intervals for ANOVA fixed- and random-effects effect sizes. *Educational and Psychological Measurement*, **61**, 575–604.

Fidler, F., Thomason, N., Cumming, G., Finch, S., & Leeman, K. (2004). Editors can lead researchers to confidence intervals, but can't make them think: Statistical reform lessons from medicine. *Psychological Science*, **15**, 119–126.

Fidler, F., Thomason, N., Cumming, G., Finch, S., & Leeman, K. (2005). Still much to learn about confidence intervals: Reply to Rouder and Morey (2005). *Psychological Science*, **16**, 494–495.

Loftus, G. R. (1993). A picture is worth a thousand p-values: On the irrelevance of hypothesis testing in the computer age. *Behavior Research Methods, Instruments, and Computers*, **25**, 250–256.

Killeen, P. R. (2005a). An alternative to null-hypothesis significance tests. *Psychological Science*, **16**, 345–353.

Killeen, P. R. (2005b). Replicability, confidence, and priors. *Psychological Science*, **16**, 1009–1012.

Loftus, G. R., & Masson, M. E. J. (1994). Using confidence intervals in within-subject designs. *Psychonomic Bulletin and Review*, **1**, 476–490.

Macdonald, R. R. (2005). Why replication probabilities depend on prior probability distributions. *Psychological Science*, **16**, 1007–1008.

Masson, M. E. J., & Loftus, G. R. (2003). Using confidence intervals for graphically based data interpretation. *Canadian Journal of Experimental Psychology*, **57**, 203–220.

McCartney, K., & Rosenthal, R. (2000). Effect size, practical importance, and social policy for children. *Child Development*, **71**, 173–180.

Olejnik, S., & Algina, J. (2003). Generalized eta and omega squared statistics: Measures of effect size for some common research designs. *Psychological Methods*, **8**, 434–447.

Rosenthal, R. (1994). Parametric measures of effect size. In H. Cooper & L. V. Hedges (Eds.), *The handbook of research synthesis* (pp. 231–244). New York: Russell Sage Foundation.

Rosenthal, R., & Rubin, D. B. (1982). A simple, general purpose display of magnitude of experimental effect. *Journal of Educational Psychology*, **74**, 166–169.

Rosnow, R. L., & Rosenthal, R. (1989). Statistical procedures and the justification of knowledge in the psychological sciences. *American Psychologist*, **44**, 1276–1284.

Rouder, J. N., & Morey, R. D. (2005). Relational and arelational confidence intervals: A comment on Fidler, Thomason, Cumming, Finch, and Leeman (2004). *Psychological Science*, **16**, 77–79.

Schmidt, F. (1996). Statistical significance testing and cumulative knowledge in psychology: Implications for training of researchers. *Psychological Methods*, **1**, 115–129.

Tabachnick, B. G., & Fidell, L. S. (2007). *Using multivariate statistics* (5th ed.). Boston, MA: Pearson Educational Inc.

Tufte, E. R. (1983). *The visual display of quantitative information*. Cheshire, CN: Graphics Press.

Tukey, J. W. (1977). *Exploratory data analysis*. Reading, MA: Addison-Wesley.

Wilkinson, L., and the Task Force on Statistical Inference. (1999). Statistical methods in psychology journals: Guidelines and explanations. *American Psychologist*, **54**, 594–604.

CONTRIBUTORS

Roger Bakeman (Ph.D., University of Texas at Austin) is professor of psychology at Georgia State University, Atlanta, Georgia. He is the author, with J. M. Gottman, of *Observing Interaction: An Introduction to Sequential Analysis* (2nd ed.; 1997), and, with V. Quera, of *Analyzing Interaction: Sequential Analysis With SDIS and GSEQ* (1995). His interests include observational methodology and sequential analysis of observational data.

Denise Brewer (Ph.D., University of North Carolina at Charlotte) is currently an Assistant Professor at Appalachian State University in the Child Development Department. She earned her Ph.D. in special education. She also received her master's degree from the University of North at Carolina Chapel Hill in early intervention and family support and her undergraduate degree from Appalachian State University in birth through kindergarten. Research interests and background include assessment issues with young children.

Kristen L. Bub (M.Ed., Harvard Graduate School of Education) is a fifth year doctoral student in Human Development and Psychology. She earned her master's degree in human development, with a concentration in research methods, from the Harvard Graduate School of Education. Her research focuses on the role that early education experiences play in children's social and academic development.

Margaret Burchinal (Ph.D., University of North Carolina) is a Senior Scientist and director of the Data Management and Analysis Center at the Frank Porter Graham Center and Research Professor of Psychology at the University of North Carolina at Chapel Hill. She is a methodologist who is best known for her methodological work on longitudinal modeling as well as for her substantive work on child care.

146

Eric Dearing (Ph.D., University of New Hampshire) is assistant professor in the Department of Counseling, Developmental, and Educational Psychology in the Lynch School of Education at Boston College. His research interests include parent–child relationships, family–school connections, child care and after-school care, and children's self-regulatory efforts in the context of family, school, and community impoverishment. He has written, taught, and been an invited speaker on the topic of applied developmental methodologies.

Lawrence C. Hamilton (Ph.D., University of Colorado at Boulder) is Professor of Sociology at the University of New Hampshire. He has written about statistical methods in articles and books such as *Modern Data Analysis* (1990), *Regression With Graphics* (1992), and six editions of *Statistics With Stata* (1990–2006). Currently, his work involves applications of analytical graphics, as well as dynamic and multilevel models to study human–environment interactions in rural communities and the circumpolar North. Hamilton has participated in national and international working groups on the human dimensions of Arctic environmental change and is a member of the Polar Research Board of the U.S. National Academies.

Richard G. Lambert (Ph.D., Georgia State University) is currently an Associate Professor in the Department of Educational Leadership at the University of North Carolina at Charlotte. He earned his Ph.D. in research, measurement, and statistics. He also holds an Ed.S. in counseling psychology from Georgia State. His research interests include the evaluation of programs for young children, applied statistics, and teacher stress.

Kathleen McCartney (Ph.D., Yale University) is the Dean at the Harvard Graduate School of Education and the Gerald S. Lesser Professor of Early Childhood Development. She is a developmental psychologist, who is best known for her research on the role of experience in development, especially research on child care.

Eloise Neebe (Ph.D., University of Rochester) is the director of data management at the Data Management and Analysis Center at the Frank Porter Graham Center. She has 15 years of experience managing data from developmental projects and is responsible for ensuring data quality for over 20 developmental projects.

Lauren Nelson (Ph.D., University of North Carolina) is a Scientist and Statistician in the Data Management and Analysis Center at the Frank Porter Graham Center and Research Assistant Professor of Psychology at the University of North Carolina at Chapel Hill. She is a methodologist who is

147

best known for serving as the statistician for the evaluation of the North Carolina pre-kindergarten program.

Michele Poe (Ph.D., Case Western Reserve University) is a Scientist and Statistician in the Data Management and Analysis Center at the Frank Porter Graham Center and Research Assistant Professor of Psychology at the University of North Carolina at Chapel Hill. She is a methodologist who is best known for her longitudinal modeling of developmental trajectories for children with rare metabolic diseases.

Keith F. Widaman (Ph.D., The Ohio State University) is Professor and Chair of the Department of Psychology at the University of California, Davis. He is a past president of the Society of Multivariate Experimental Psychology (SMEP) and received the Cattell Award from SMEP for early career contributions to multivariate psychology. His substantive research interests include the structure, development, and cognitive processes underlying mental abilities, the development of adaptive behavioral skills by persons with mental retardation, and the ways in which genes and environmental agents influence behavioral development within family contexts. His quantitative interests include correlation/regression analysis, common factor analysis, and structural equation modeling, especially factorial invariance and the analysis of multitrait–multimethod data.

STATEMENT OF EDITORIAL POLICY

The *Monographs* series is devoted to publishing developmental research that generates authoritative new findings and uses these to foster fresh, better integrated, or more coherent perspectives on major developmental issues, problems, and controversies. The significance of the work in extending developmental theory and contributing definitive empirical information in support of a major conceptual advance is the most critical editorial consideration. Along with advancing knowledge on specialized topics, the series aims to enhance cross-fertilization among developmental disciplines and developmental sub fields. Therefore, clarity of the links between the specific issues under study and questions relating to general developmental processes is important. These links, as well as the manuscript as a whole, must be as clear to the general reader as to the specialist. The selection of manuscripts for editorial consideration, and the shaping of manuscripts through reviews-and-revisions, are processes dedicated to actualizing these ideals as closely as possible.

Typically *Monographs* entail programmatic large-scale investigations; sets of programmatic interlocking studies; or—in some cases—smaller studies with highly definitive and theoretically significant empirical findings. Multi-authored sets of studies that center on the same underlying question can also be appropriate; a critical requirement here is that all studies address common issues, and that the contribution arising from the set as a whole be unique, substantial, and well integrated. The needs of integration preclude having individual chapters identified by individual authors. In general, irrespective of how it may be framed, any work that is judged to significantly extend developmental thinking will be taken under editorial consideration.

To be considered, submissions should meet the editorial goals of *Monographs* and should be no briefer than a minimum of 80 pages (including references and tables). There is an upper limit of 175–200 pages. In exceptional circumstances this upper limit may be modified. (Please submit four copies.) Because a *Monograph* is inevitably lengthy and usually substantively complex, it is particularly important that the text be well organized and written in clear, precise, and literate English. Note, however, that authors from non-English-speaking countries should not be put off by this stricture. In accordance with the general aims of SRCD, this series is actively interested in promoting international exchange of developmental research. Neither membership in the Society nor affiliation with the academic discipline of psychology are relevant in considering a *Monographs* submission.

The corresponding author for any manuscript must, in the submission letter, warrant that all coauthors are in agreement with the content of the manuscript. The corresponding author also is responsible for informing all coauthors, in a timely manner, of manuscript submission, editorial decisions, reviews received, and any revisions recommended. Before publication, the corresponding author also must warrant in the submission letter that the study has been conducted according to the ethical guidelines of the Society for Research in Child Development.

Potential authors who may be unsure whether the manuscript they are planning would make an appropriate submission are invited to draft an outline of what they propose, and send it to the Editor for assessment. This mechanism, as well as a more detailed description of all editorial policies, evaluation process, and format requirements can be found at the Editorial Office website (http://astro.temple.edu/-overton/monosrcd.html) or by contacting the Editor, Wills F. Overton, Temple University-Psychology, 1701 North 13th St. – Rm 567, Philadelphia, PA 19122-6085 (e-mail: monosrcd@temple.edu) (telephone: 1-215-204-7360).

Monographs of the Society for Research in Child Development (ISSN 0037-976X), one of two publications of Society of Research in Child Development, is published three times a year by Blackwell Publishing with offices at 350 Main St., Malden, MA 02148 and PO Box 1354, Garsington Rd, Oxford, OX4 2DQ, UK and PO Box 378 Carlton South, 3053 Victoria, Australia. A subscription to *Monographs of the SRCD* comes with a subscription to *Child Development* (published bimonthly).

INFORMATION FOR SUBSCRIBERS For new orders, renewals, sample copy requests, claims, changes of address and all other subscription correspondences please contact the Journals Department at your nearest Blackwell office (address details listed above). UK office phone: +44 (0) 1865-778315, Fax: +44 (0) 1865-471775, Email: customerservices@ blackwellpublishing.com; US office phone: 800-835-6770 or 781-388-8599, Fax: 781-388-8232, Email: customerservices@blackwellpublishing.com; Asia office phone: +65 6511 8000, Fax: +61 3 8359 1120, Email: customerservices@blackwellpublishing.com

INSTITUTIONAL PREMIUM RATES* FOR MONOGRAPHS OF THE SRCD/CHILD DEVELOPMENT 2005 The Americas $471, Rest of World £335. Customers in Canada should add 7% GST to The Americas price or provide evidence of entitlement to exemption. Customers in the UK and EU should add VAT at 5% or provide a VAT registration number or evidence of entitlement to exemption.

*A Premium Institutional Subscription includes online access to full text articles from 1997 to present, where available. Print and online-only rates are also available.

BACK ISSUES Back issues are available from the publisher at the current single issue rate.

MICROFORM The journal is available on microfilm. For microfilm service, address inquiries to ProQuest Information and Learning, 300 North Zeeb Road, Ann Arbor, MI 48106-1346, USA. Bell and Howell Serials Customer Service Department: (800) 521-0600 × 2873.

MAILING Periodical postage paid at Boston, MA and additional offices. Mailing to rest of world by DHL Smart & Global Mail. Canadian mail is sent by Canadian publications mail agreement number 40573520. Postmaster: Send all address changes to *Monographs of the Society for Research in Child Development*, Blackwell Publishing Inc., Journals Subscription Department, 350 Main St., Malden, MA 02148-5020.

 Sign up to receive Blackwell *Synergy* free e-mail alerts with complete *Monographs of the SRCD* tables of contents and quick links to article abstracts from the most current issue. Simply go to www.blackwell synergy.com, select the journal from the list of journals, and click on "Sign-up" for FREE email table of contents alerts.

CURRENT